Ask the Family

KU-739-814

How many questions on *Ask the Family* could you
answer? Do you think the contestants brilliant, or are
you amazed at their lack of general knowledge?

Now you can find out how successful your family
would be without leaving home. Here are hundreds of
questions (and their answers too) from the television
programmes. The forty quizzes are arranged by subject
matter, and there are illustrations and a photo-quiz.
The first *Ask the Family* book provided hours of
enjoyment, and quiz enthusiasts everywhere will
welcome this completely new selection.

Ask the Family 2

questions and answers from
the BBC tv quiz game

illustrated by Nigel Holmes

British Broadcasting Corporation

Ask the Family has been running for eight years
on BBC 1 with Robert Robinson as
compère and Cecil Korer as producer.

Published by the
British Broadcasting Corporation
35 Marylebone High Street
London W1M 4AA

ISBN 0 563 12231 5

First published 1972, reprinted 1973, 1975 (twice)

Printed in England by Hunt Barnard Printing Ltd
Aylesbury, Bucks

Contents

1 General Knowledge 1

1 If Norfolk's is a castle in Sussex, where is Devonshire's?

2 What is the 'city of brotherly love', founded in 1682, called today?

3 Where would you want no wow or flutter in your tweeter and woofer?

4 Under what circumstances could you visit Belfast and not leave London?

5 Where can one find a hare's foot and a stag's horn which have no connection with an animal?

6 According to Acton Bell, where did 'the tenant' live?

7 Which English cathedral has: (a) As many pillars as there are hours in a year, (b) The same number of windows as there are days in a year?

8 What district of London is a 19th-century historian?

9 There are four small independent states in Europe, each with a population of about 20,000. Three of them are the principalities of Andorra, Liechtenstein and Monaco, but the fourth is a republic. It has Pluto, Goofie and Mickey Mouse on its stamps. What is it?

10 Who, in London, is over 17 ft tall at over 170 ft from the ground?

11 Who continues this series: Davidson, Lang, Temple, Fisher?

12 What is the connection between Copenhagen, Marengo, and a London railway station?

13 What connection have heart's ease and love-in-idleness with a French word for thought?

14 Which bridge is missing in this sequence of London road bridges over the Thames: Chelsea, Albert, Battersea, Putney, Hammersmith?

2 Number Quiz 1

1 What are the three positive numbers whose sum equals their product?

2 Which is the most economical size of washing-up liquid to buy if it is sold in the following sizes: (a) Small, 12½ oz. @ 8p, (b) Large, 14½ oz. @ 10p, (c) Family, 19½ oz. @ 13p?

3 Which of the following solutions is the correct one:

$$\frac{\text{MDCCLXIV}}{\text{XIV}} = \begin{array}{ll} \text{(a)} & \text{LXXXVI} \\ \text{(b)} & \text{CXIV} \\ \text{(c)} & \text{CXXVI} \\ \text{(d)} & \text{CXVI?} \end{array}$$

4 If I buy four lengths of wire 12 ft 6 in. long; six lengths 14 ft 4 in. long and eight lengths 9 ft 3 in. long, how many yards of wire will I have?

5 What is the ninth letter before Q?

6 If a car does 25 miles per gallon of petrol, how many kilometres per litre is that?

7 Can you find the difference between Union and League, multiply it by Association and add Shakespeare's ages of man?

8 How often in a twelve-month period do consecutive months have 31 days?

9 If an old clock gains five minutes an hour, and it is put right at midnight, what time will it be when it says ten past three in the afternoon?

10 The rungs of a 21-rung ladder are 6 in. apart. The top and bottom rungs are 1 ft from the ends. How long is the ladder?

11 An agent sold an old cottage for £1,500. On the first £600 he charged 5% commission and on the remainder 3%. How much commission did he collect?

12 What is the square root of 20% of 50% of 75% of 120?

13 If a girl of nine is three times as old as her brother, how long will it be before she is twice as old?

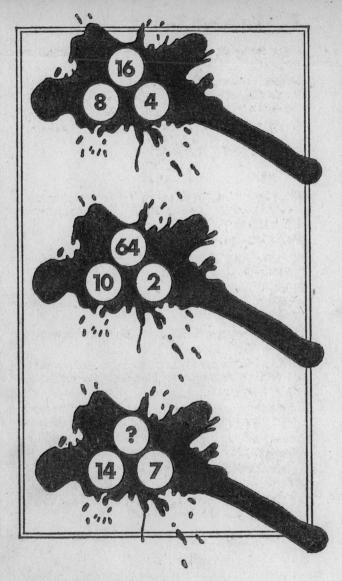

14 What is the missing figure?

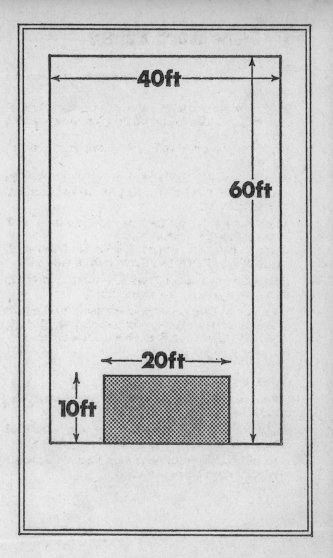

15 The drawing represents a lawn and patio, which is shaded. How many 2-ft-square turfs would be needed to cover the unshaded part?

3 Some Word Games

1 A VUISETNRNIAA.
In this anagram can you remove the capital and leave the country?

2 Which word means: (a) A famous father, (b) A kind of overcoat, (c) A town in Derbyshire, (d) A heavily padded sofa?

3 Which three words, sounding the same, mean: 'water', 'rule' and 'strap'?

4 What are the following words beginning with 'bat': (a) Anticlimax, (b) Peculiar to cricket, (c) Liquid in cooking, (d) Robin's friend?

5 Which two words, sounding the same, mean 'to look narrowly', 'nobility' and 'structure'?

6 Which of the following words is mis-spelt: 'deleterious', 'irremediable', 'skillfull', 'expediential' and 'eximious'?

7 What letter of the alphabet connects a female domestic animal, a pronoun and an evergreen tree?

8 From each of these groups of letters two words may be formed except in one case where only one is possible: ABD, DNO, SWA, IPN, UNP. Which is the odd one out?

9 Can you solve (b) by analogy?
 (a) PARTY (TODAY) DEVON
 (b) SEDAN (-----) HOUSE

10 Can you take away a Spanish artist and leave a French one: MPAITCIASSSSEO?

11 Which church dignitary can also be a number, a small red bird and a flower of the Lobelia family?

12 What are these two words? Across is a peninsula; down is a weather condition experienced there.

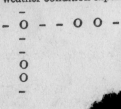

A E I
E I M
I M ?

13 What is the missin

14 Can you transpose two letters in the word 'united' to get a word with the opposite meaning?

15 In this family of 'cats', can you name the ones that are: (a) A raft or float of logs, or of two boats, tied side by side, (b) A weapon used in ancient wars or by modern boys, (c) A sudden disaster?

16 What do these words have in common: 'man', 'child', 'ox', and 'woman'?

4 People in Fact and Fiction

1 What are the surnames of these families of children and in which books do they occur: (a) Wendy, John and Michael, (b) Tom, Mary and Sidney, (c) Ernest, Fritz, Jack and Franz (or Francis)?

2 What were the christian names of the fictional family whose surname is the third month of the year?

3 Which Shakespearian character is a European capital?

4 Who spoke the following words and where: 'That's one small step for a man, one giant leap for mankind'?

5 For what do the initials stand for in the following: (a) Percy B. Shelley, (b) Ulysses S. Grant, (c) William T. Sherman?

6 Where will you find the Duke of Brontë, guarded by four Landseer lions?

7 Which unusual christian name is shared by a character in the radio programme *The Archers* and one in the children's television programme *The Magic Roundabout*?

8 Which American poet and English author might each be connected with wintry weather?

9 Who received twelve diamond studs as a present from her husband, and to whom did she give them?

10 Who were the following: (a) Much, (b) Shallow, (c) Small?

11 Whose middle names were these: (a) Ewart, (b) Langhorne, (c) Lutwidge, (d) Fingall O'Flahertie Wills?

12 Who removed a specimen of *Prunus domestica* on the tip of his first phalange and what was his comment?

13 Can you complete the following trios: (a) Aldrin, Armstrong and ?, (b) Ham, Shem and ?, (c) Peter, Paul and ?, (d) Wynken, Blynken and ?

14 For what is Joseph Lister famous?

15 By what names were or are the following known: (a) Rodrigo or Ruydiaz, (b) Henry I of England, (c) Josip Broz, (d) Iosif Vissarionovich Dzhugashvili?

16 What valuable fruit caused a Spanish princess to pay a social call?

17 If Goldilocks and the Three Bears threw a tea party and invited the Seven Dwarfs, Tweedledum and Tweedledee, Old Mother Hubbard and Simple Simon, how many females would be present?

18 Of whose epitaph is this the end and where would one find it: *... they buried him among the Kings because he had done good towards God and towards his house?*

5 Geographical Quiz

1 In what country are the initial letters of the counties FAT LAD?

2 Which is the nearest to the equator: London, New York, Montreal or Rome?

3 If one sailed due west from Land's End where would one first touch land?

4 Which of the following is the best reason for the North Pole being colder than the Equator: (a) The North Pole is further from the sun, (b) There is more ice there, (c) The sun's rays fall more obliquely?

5 *By the shining big sea water,*
  Stood the wigwam of Nokomis. . . .
  By which shore did it stand?

6 What is the modern name of the promontory which was previously known as *Cabo Tormentoso* (the Stormy Cape), Lion of the Sea and Head of Africa?

7 What location have Queen Mary Land (or Coast) and Queen Maud Land in common?

8 Which country is made up of Serbia, Croatia, Montenegro, Bosnia, Herzegovina, Slovenia and Macedonia?

9 There is another 'London' on another River 'Thames', which is not in England. Where is it?

10 If one were to board a ship at Reykjavik and sail due south, where would one first strike land?

11 Which is the shorter distance by air from London: Dublin or Amsterdam?

12 What Commonwealth island outside the British Isles is comprised of the three counties: Cornwall, Surrey and Middlesex?

13 If a man sails a boat due east from the Thames Estuary, which country will he reach?

14 Which is the farthest distance from London by air: Bermuda, Toronto or Nairobi?

6 General Knowledge 2

1 If the Czar comes first, followed by Pershore (both in August), with Victoria a month later, what would you do with them?

2 At the moment it is 4 ft 8½ in. though Brunel wanted it to be 7 ft ¼ in. What is it?

3 Who painted the ceiling of the Sistine Chapel in the Vatican?

4 What are the following articles of dress and why are they so named: (a) A belcher, (b) A spencer, (c) A trilby?

5 Which of the following activities uses up the most calories per hour: (a) Rowing at 33 strokes per minute, (b) Running at 7½ mph, (c) Bicycling at 13 mph?

6 Why do London, Warrington, Lancashire Lad and Bedford Red all make delicious pies?

7 Who were Clotho, Lachesis and Atropos?

8 What operations in World War II did the following code names stand for: (a) Operation Torch, (b) Operation Sealion, (c) Operation Overlord, (d) Operation Mulberry?

9 What are Cygnus, Boötes, Ursa Major and Corona Borealis?

10 Which is the missing date in the following: ? ; 17 March; 23 April and 30 November?

11 What pop groups sound like: (a) A late-night drink, (b) A double white line, (c) A breakfast spread?

12 Approximately 314 million people throughout the world speak English. Which language is spoken by more people?

13 The date given for the deaths of Shakespeare and Cervantes is the same – 23 April 1616 – but they did not die on the same day. Why?

14 What was first known around the fourth century BC, has a geographical origin in south-western Asia, the scientific name of *Malus Pumila*, and can be cooked or eaten raw?

15 When you go through a door, on which side are the hinges?

16 What is this bridge called and where is it?

7 Anagrams

1 SEEMS ROT
An unfortunate anagram for the middle name of an English author.

2 IT MEANS TOIL.
It will, if it gets you the job.

3 NINE THUMPS.
It speaks for itself.

4 NEAR ANCIENT.
You certainly are, if you're this.

5 ADAM'S GIRL.
Melodious birds sing them.

6 THE CLASSROOM.
This is an anagram very applicable to the occupier.

7 NAY I REPENT IT.
If you do, you won't end up here again.

8 HAS TO PILFER.
In order to be one.

9 MEATS? I'VE GRAIN.
Nut cutlets.

10 A HOME FOR UPSET NAILS.
People who go there get elected.

11 EGGS TO BEER.
This footballer trains on one rather than the other.

12 I HIRE PARSONS.
I hire them for these people.

13 MATCH IS TAME.
This could help with the scoring.

14 A DOUR NEED.
It was one up to Marlborough.

8   Number Quiz 2

1 If, by a merging of time and space, you had to book seats for the Apostles, the Musketeers, the Just Men, the Stooges, the Lily White Boys, and the Ladies Dancing, how many would you need to reserve?

2 If you multiplied the number of feet in two yards by the number of pints in a gallon and subtracted the answer from the number of weeks in a year, what would the answer be?

3 How many spots are there on six dice?

4 What is a third minus a quarter?

5 What is the sum of the first four prime numbers above ten?

6 A man is now three times as old as his son. In 15 years' time he will only be twice as old. What are their present ages?

7 I walk along one side of a square field and I have then walked 180 yards less than if I had walked round it. What is the area of the field?

8 There are three lights next to each other and one flashes every four seconds, another every six seconds and the third every eight seconds. If they are started together, how long will it be before they have all flashed simultaneously five more times?

9 What is $\frac{3}{2}$ minus $\frac{2}{3}$?

10 What is the square root of the sum of the digits in the year of the Battle of El Alamein?

11 When does 12 equal 5?

12 A is half a mile north of B, B is half a mile east of C and C is half a mile south of D. In what direction is D from A?

13 How would you arrange these numbers in two piles so that both piles total the same, and what would the total of each pile be?

$$
\begin{array}{cccc}
8 & 6 & 2 & 3 \\
7 & 5 & 1 & 4
\end{array}
$$

+ =30p

+ =40p

+ =50p

14 What is the value of the fruit?

pineapple = 10p

Ban = 20p

Pear = 80p

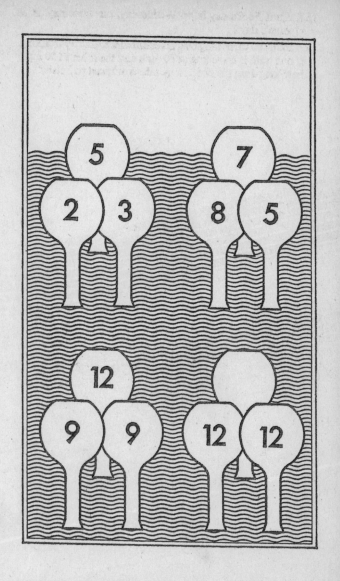

15 What is the missing number?

16 If April Fool's day is on Wednesday, on what day is St George's day?

17 A train 100 yards long overtakes another train 76 yards long. If one train is travelling at 60 mph and the other at 50 mph, how long does the overtaking take from start to finish?

9 Odd Man Out

1 Which of these is the odd one out: (a) Charles Ross, (b) Prince Albert, (c) Lord Derby, (d) Lloyd George, (e) James Grieve?

2 Which is the odd one out: amber, ruby, coral, jet and pearl?

3 Which is the odd flag out: Holland, Sweden, W. Germany and Austria?

4 Which is the odd one out: Exodus, Psalms, Jeremiah, Hezekiah, Malachi?

5 Which is the odd one out: Everest, Etna, Table, Eiger?

6 Which is the odd one out: Shetland Isles, Hebrides, Faeroes, Orkney?

7 Which of these is the odd one out?

10 More Word Games

1 Which two words, sounding the same, are associated with: 'a seat of authority', 'to perceive' and 'salt water'?

2 What is the essential difference between a bathysphere and a bathyscaphe?

3 What do the following initials stand for: (a) DORA, (b) ENSA, (c) NAAFI, (d) OCTU, (e) PLUTO, (f) RADAR?

4 Which three words, sounding the same, mean: 'a formal procedure'; 'to make symbols', 'a direction'?

5 (a) BEACH (CHART) RITES
  (b) CRATE (-----) MISTY
  Can you solve (b) by analogy?

6 What word describes a range of mountains, a figure in Greek mythology and a work of reference?

7 What do these have in common: 'helicopter', 'pterodactyl' and 'chapter'?

8 What ancient capital city is an anagram of the present-day capital?

9 (a) THEIR (ISLET) CLASP
  (b) ECLAT (-----) SPUME
  Can you solve (b) by analogy?

10 What three words, sounding the same, mean: 'to encounter', 'food', 'to measure'?

11 Can you complete the following to form three well-known phrases:
  (a) --ITY   --ITY
  (b) --KEY   --KEY
  (c) -OI   -OLLO-?

12 Can you think of five different four-letter words with 'AS' in the middle?

13 What are the full Latin expressions of the following abbreviations and what are their meanings: (a) i.e., (b) e.g., (c) viz., (d) q.v.?

14 Which words beginning with 'coll' mean: (a) 'work together', (b) 'side by side', (c) 'secret agreement'?

15 Which two words with the same sounds are associated with 'dogs', 'trees' and 'water'?

16 The down clue is a religious festival and the across clue a famous naval battle of World War II. Can you fill in the missing letters?

11 Religious Quiz

1 Which festivals have changed places in the following sequence: Advent / Epiphany / Christmas / Lent / Easter / Whitsun?

2 Which two biblical characters are reminiscent of an auction?

3 What church dignitary always has his robe back to front?

4 Which of these books of the Bible is in the New Testament: (a) Micah, (b) Titus, (c) Joel, (d) Amos?

5 Which biblical character is associated with a jawbone and bees?

6 If St Augustine was the first, who is the hundredth?

7 What is missing from this list of the books of Moses: Genesis, Exodus, Leviticus and Numbers?

8 Who was the first High Priest of the Jews?

9 Who wrote: 'I look upon all the world as my Parish'?

10 On which Mediterranean island was St Paul shipwrecked?

12 General Knowledge 3

1 If a country shows its Latin name *Helvetia* on its postage stamps, what will the initials be on its car insignia?

2 These three books were all written by ex-Prime Ministers: who were the authors? (a) *Full Circle*, (b) *My Early Life*, (c) *The Blast of War*.

3 What is wheaten paste called when formed into slender, worm-like threads?

4 What relation to you is the only son of your father's father?

5 What are these: Red Gauntlet, Talisman, Hampshire Maid, Royal Sovereign and Cambridge Vigour?

6 What is the trial of Pyx?

7 To what are the following descriptions applicable: (a) A picture made by arranging small pieces of stone in different colours, (b) A picture made by printing from a metal plate which has been partly eaten away by acids?

8 What does this jingle describe:
Two birds, flying high,
A chinese vessel, sailing by,
A bridge with three men, sometimes four,
A weeping willow, hanging o'er,
A Chinese temple, there it stands
Built upon the river sands.
An apple tree, with apples on,
A crooked fence, to end, my son?

9 Who made Salford famous?

10 Andrew, Brian and Charles were a mile out at sea in a boat when a rifle was fired on shore in their direction. Andrew only heard the report of the gun, Brian only saw the flash, and Charles merely saw the bullet strike the water near them. Which of them first knew of the discharge of the rifle?

11 Which French painter made the South Sea Islands famous?

12 What have the following towns in common: Cranford, Casterbridge and Villette?

13 Which letter of the alphabet is always missing from a telephone?

14 What have the following in common: painted, red, swallow, Camberwell?

15 Who painted Whistler's mother?

16 What connection, other than meteorological, have tornado, typhoon, tempest and hurricane?

17 What have Oxford, London, a hen, a clock and a miracle in common?

13 Literature

1 Who is the odd one out: Mr and Mrs Snagsby; Augustus Snodgrass; Count Smorltork?

2 Who were the wives of the following Shakespearian characters: (a) Oberon, (b) Antony, (c) Caesar, (d) Othello, (e) Leontes?

3 Under what name did Mrs Montague Barstow write her books?

4 The following detectives attend the Annual Detectives' Dinner Dance: Paul Temple, Hercule Poirot, Simon Templar, Miss Marple, Gideon of the Yard and the Baron. If their creators were also invited, which writers would turn up?

5 Which of the Brontë sisters was: (a) Acton, (b) Currer, (c) Ellis?

6 Who wrote about the following families: (a) The Herries, (b) The Forsytes, (c) The Marches, (d) The Pleydells (known as Berry & Co.)?

7 Who lived at the following places: (a) Manderley, (b) Haworth Parsonage, (c) Lissom Grove?

8 Which famous author is referred to in the following description: Born in Paris 1874 of Irish origin, and educated in England. He qualified as a surgeon at St Thomas's Hospital, London. In 1914 he served with a Red Cross unit in France, then as a secret agent in Geneva. A British agent in World War II, he fled from France in 1940 with only a suitcase and lived until 1946 in the USA. He spent two years in a Scottish tuberculosis sanatorium.

9 In which books do the following characters appear: (a) First Lieutenant Eccles, (b) Joseph Sedley, (c) Squire Trelawney?

10 Which author's eightieth book was published on her eightieth birthday?

11 Who wrote the following: (a) *The Last Days of Pompeii*, (b) *Rip Van Winkle*, (c) *She Stoops to Conquer*, (d) *Ingoldsby Legends*?

14 Kings and Queens

1 Which monarch reigned during the Great Plague and the Great Fire of London?

2 How long did Harold II reign before William the Conqueror came to the throne?

3 At Smithfield in 1381, the peasants roared, 'They have slain our Captain.' A boy of 14 answered, 'I am your Captain and your King, follow me.' Who was the slain Captain and who the King?

4 Who were the first and last monarchs of these houses: (a) Plantagenets, (b) Tudors, (c) Hanover?

5 Who married the following: (a) Mary of Teck, (b) Mary of Modena, (c) Catherine of Braganza, (d) George of Denmark?

6 What was the relationship between the following: (a) George II and his successor, George III, (b) William IV and his successor, Queen Victoria?

7 Which British monarch reigned during the American Civil War?

8 Which Stuart sovereign is commemorated by a monument in Westminster Abbey?

9 If Elizabeth II is the sixth, who were the other five?

10 Which four English kings reigned between Edward III (1327-77) and Edward IV (1461-83)?

11 Can you name in their correct order the wives of Henry VIII?

12 Who were the Norman kings of England?

13 Which two kings reigned between Harold I and Harold II?

14 What is the link between Edward V and Edward VIII, Kings of England?

15 Number Quiz 3

1 If 128 teams entered a knock-out football competition, how many games would the winning team play?

2 A 1-lb. bag of flour weighs 1 lb. 0 oz. The carton into which the bags are packed holds two dozen bags and weighs 1 lb. The delivery van can hold 100 cartons. What weight of flour is the van carrying when fully laden?

3 How many cubic feet of earth are there in a hole 4′ × 5′ × 6′?

4 A man is now seven times as old as his son. In ten years' time he will be only three times as old. What are their present ages?

5 Tom can run faster than Bill. Bill is not so fast as Joe, and Joe is not so fast as Tom. Who runs most slowly?

6 You are going to visit some children. You don't know how many, but not more than six. What is the smallest number of sweets you can take and be sure of being able to divide them equally among the children?

7 A train, which is 110 yards long and travelling at 30 mph, goes through a tunnel which is 770 yards long. How much time will elapse between the front of the train going into the tunnel and the back coming out?

8 How many $\frac{1}{4}$-in. markings are there in a 6-ft rule marked in tenths of an inch?

9 What is the sum of all the even numbers from 0 to 20?

10 What is $1^1 + 2^2 + 3^3 + 4^4$?

11 If 3 June is a Monday, on what day does 31 June fall?

12 Five airlines, each running 100-seater planes, run services across an ocean with an average daily total seat occupancy of 40%. If on one average day, four of the planes hold 50 passengers each, how many passengers are in the fifth?

13 In a 30-lap race, the leader lapped in $8\frac{1}{2}$ minutes, and the tailender in 10 minutes. How far behind was the tailender when the leader crossed the finishing line?

14 What is the missing number?

15 What is the missing number?

16
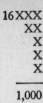

1,000

What is X?

17 Three brothers, Tom, Bill and Dan, eat a regular quantity of apples every day. Tom eats twice as many as Dan; Bill eats three-quarters as many as Tom; Dan eats two apples a day. How many apples are consumed by the brothers in a week?

16 History

1 Which Scottish leader was executed in London in 1305?

2 In Robert Southey's well-known poem starting:
It was a summer evening,
Old Kaspar's work was done,
And he before his cottage door
Was sitting in the sun
The last line is *But 'twas a famous victory*. Which battle was it?

3 In what incident is it estimated that some 13,200 houses, over 80 churches, 400 streets were destroyed, but less than 10 people lost their lives?

4 Who is missing from this list: Victoria, Alexandra, Lionheart, Edward, Albert, Berengaria and Arthur?

5 Which of the following events did not happen in a year ending with 15: (a) the signing of Magna Carta, (b) the death of Shakespeare, (c) the battle of Waterloo, (d) the Jacobite Rebellion?

6 Who was one of the earliest undergraduates at Harvard, urged Cromwell to accept the throne, was knighted by Charles II, and now has a famous London street named after him?

7 What Act of Parliament, applying particularly to Scotsmen, was passed after the Jacobite Rebellion of 1745 and repealed in 1782?

8 In the Crimean War the Battle of Balaclava gave its name to an article of wearing apparel – the Balaclava helmet. What two other articles of clothing have the same names as two of the commanders at the same battle?

9 Apart from being Prime Ministers, what did Pitt the younger and James Balfour have in common with Edward Heath?

10 In which reigns did the following events happen: (a) The Battle of Shrewsbury, where Hotspur died, (b) The burning of Joan of Arc. (c) The death of Wat Tyler?

11 In the following chronological sequence, which houses have been transposed: Norman, Plantagenet, York, Lancaster, Tudor, Stuart, Hanover, Saxe-Coburg and Windsor?

12 Who was born the daughter of a prince of the house of Anhalt-Zerbst, at Stettin on 2 May 1729, and christened Sophie Augusta Frederika?

13 What is the connection between: Naseby, Edge Hill, Marston Moor?

14 What were the dates of the following battles: (a) Preston Pans, (b) Agincourt, (c) Austerlitz, (d) Worcester, (e) Trafalgar?

15 How many Prime Ministers have there been so far during the reign of Elizabeth II?

16 Which year saw the birth of the Parliamentary Labour Party; the relief of Ladysmith; the publication of George Bernard Shaw's *Captain Brassbound's Conversion;* the completion of Puccini's *Tosca,* and the first flight by a German Zeppelin airship?

17 Sporting Interlude

1 With which game are the following terms connected: Bean ball; Charley Horse; and Foot in the bucket?

2 Which league in British football has an odd number of teams, and how many are there?

3 In snooker, when all the red balls have been pocketed, how many points are left on the table?

4 Can you make one English football team out of two Scottish ones?

5 All the following men have been footballers of the year: Frank McLintock (Arsenal), Billy Bremner (Leeds United), Tony Book (Manchester City) and Dave McKay (Derby County). What else had they in common?

6 What sporting activity do you associate with the following places: (a) Murrayfield, (b) Madison Square Gardens, (c) Badminton, (d) Forest Hills, (e) Wrigley Field?

7 What piece of wearing apparel connects the following sportsmen: Trevor Legett; Gunji Koizumi; Geoffrey Gleeson; John Newman and Mikonosuke Kawaishi?

8 Can you think of three sports in which the competitors are moving backwards when they win?

9 What sports do you associate with the following: (a) The Americas Cup, (b) The Davis Cup, (c) The Calcutta Cup, (d) The Gold Cup?

10 (a) What English sport was prohibited in England by Oliver Cromwell in 1653 and by Parliament in 1849? (b) In which country is it still a pastime?

11 What are the nicknames of the following rugby teams: (a) The Australian rugby team, (b) The New Zealand rugby team, (c) The British rugby team?

12 How many players are there in the following teams: (a) A baseball team, (b) A lacrosse team, (c) A netball team?

13 What sports do the following terms come from: (a) In the gold, (b) The diamond, (c) Bully-off, (d) The twenty-five, (e) Boston Crab?

14 What umpired game has five forwards, three halfbacks, two full backs and a goalkeeper?

15 If the Owls competed against the Magpies at the home of the Peacocks, who would be concerned and where?

16 What do the football teams of Southampton, Perth and Paisley have in common with Simon Templar?

18   More Anagrams

1 FINE, BRING HOT.
Advice to Guy Fawkes.

2 HOW SAD IT CAN BE.
Something Parliamentary.

3 KEEP A MACE.
A literary middle name or it could be an ultimate deterrent.

4 MEN ARE TRAINED.
Rather a salty one.

5 NOT MUSE VERSE.
Because it's there.

6 CHEAPER? I RUSH.
Not if I bought this way?

7 MEN TEST A DRIVE.
And publicise the result.

8 A GRIM ERA.
And it's supposed to be blissful.

9 NICER NIGHTS.
He who gets splashed.

10 PEPYS SAID.
When asked what he was suffering from.

11 RAMON IS PIOUS.
However, he can be mean.

12 CAN'T PASS TO TRAINS.
It must be rush hour here.

13 HOMELY STAR SETS.
Both this and the answer are astronomical.

19 River Quiz

1 Which river ran 'through caverns measureless to man'?

2 What do the Rivers Nene, Welland, Witham and Ouse flow into?

3 Which river was asked, 'run softly till I end my song'?

4 Which river washes, on the southern side, the walls of a once infested city?

5 Which river did Huckleberry Finn sail down in a raft?

6 What river sounds like a number?

7 Which river is the 'one more river to cross'?

8 On which river 'lived a jolly miller once'?

9 Which river flows quietly?

10 Which river was 'grey, green, greasy, all set about with fever trees'?

11 In which countries do these rivers have their source: (a) River Rhine, (b) River Danube, (c) River Euphrates, (d) River Amazon?

20 General Knowledge 4

1 In 1947 David Winter submitted two of his paintings to the Royal Academy. In England he was known as a famous bricklayer amongst other things. Who was he?

2 In which cities are the following art galleries: (a) The Prado, (b) The Rijksmuseum, (c) The Uffizi, (d) The Metropolitan Museum of Art?

3 From what plant sources are the following derived: (a) Morphine, (b) Quinine, (c) Cocaine?

4 Apart from the sun, which is the next nearest star to the earth?

5 Which painter was famous for his paintings of ballet and horses?

6 Which countries are associated with these airlines: (a) Sabena, (b) Qantas, (c) K.L.M., (d) S.A.S., (e) El Al, (f) Aeroflot?

7 What do the stripes on the United States flag stand for, and how many are there?

8 Under what expert conditions does a minute last longer than just one minute?

9 What is 12 or 8 in England and Wales; 12 or 15 in Scotland and 12 or 7 in Northern Ireland?

10 The words 'closure', 'gag', 'guillotine' and 'kangaroo' all refer to the same thing. What is it?

11 If you have specimens of Dead Men's Ropes, Peacocks' Tails, Balloons, Green Laver, Bladder Wrack and Toothed Rack, what do you collect?

12 What runs 'forrard' on the starboard side of a ship and 'aft' on the port side?

13 In Russian *Belka* means 'squirrel' and *Strelka* means 'little arrow'. But what were they and what happened to them?

14 What is missing from this list: Oscar Wilde, Spandau, Edmund Dantés, Dreyfus, Reading Gaol, Devil's Island, Rudolf Hess?

21 Unlikely Connections

1 What two garments are also islands?

2 What is the connection between the original name of the island of which Haiti forms approximately one-third, and R. L. Stevenson's *Treasure Island*?

3 What have the following in common: (a) John Evelyn and Samuel Pepys, (b) The *Titanic* and the R.101, (c) John Milton and Pew?

4 What is the connection between the following: tub, companion, balloon back, vespers?

5 What is the connection between a 17th-century poet, a 20th-century economist and a new city?

6 Which measure of length can swim?

7 What can be found in architecture, carpentry and cloth as well as in a fish?

8 What name connects: (a) A pickled herring, (b) A sunken battleship, (c) A German Chancellor?

9 What game is also a drink?

10 What is the connection between the following: farmhouse, cottage, sandwich, Vienna, bloomer, Coburg?

11 What tree is connected with the seaside?

12 What name connects John, an English preacher and writer, with Paul the mythical hero of American folklore?

13 What connection have these with a maritime safety measure?

22 Number Quiz 4

1 If two cars are 30 miles apart approaching each other on a motorway, and they are both travelling at 45 mph, how long will it be before they pass each other?

2 The blind mice, the kittens who lost their mittens and the blackbirds baked in a pie went to celebrate the wedding of the owl and the pussycat. (a) How many were present? (b) How many legs between them?

3 Who will cover a 150 yards' course more quickly, a man who goes 3 yards per second all the way, or one who goes 4 yards per second for 100 yards and 2 yards per second for the remaining 50 yards?

4 In Roman numerals, five of the figures between one and ten begin with the same letter. What is the sum of the remainder?

5 How much is twice half two and a half?

6 In American packets of cigarettes the 20 cigarettes are usually arranged in three rows, whilst British cigarettes are in two rows. If cigarettes are $\frac{1}{4}$ inch in diameter, how much wider is a British pack than an American pack?

7 What is $2^8 - 8^2$?

8 If 26 May is a Wednesday, what day is 10 June, the same year?

9 If $\frac{3}{4}$ of a number is greater by 12 than $\frac{2}{5}$ of the number, what is the number?

10 If a driver is travelling at 30 mph and his reaction time is $\frac{3}{4}$ of a second, how far will he have travelled by the time he applies his brakes?

11 If time were decimalised so that there were 100 new seconds to the new minute, 100 new minutes to the new hour and 10 new hours to the day, would the old second or the new one be longer?

12 What is 50% of 25% of 20% of £1?

13 How many minutes is it until 9 o'clock if forty minutes ago it was three times as many minutes past 7 o'clock?

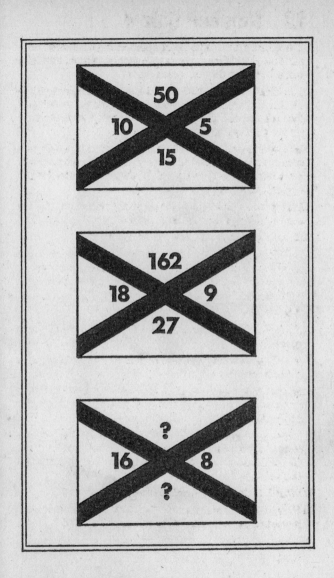

14 What are the missing numbers?

15 What number is represented on the top face of this dice?

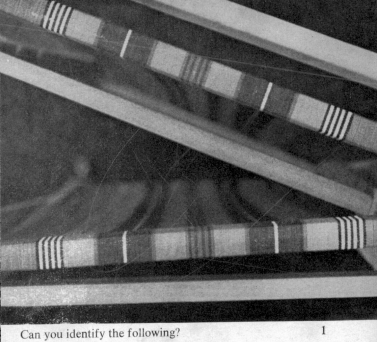

Can you identify the following?

1

2

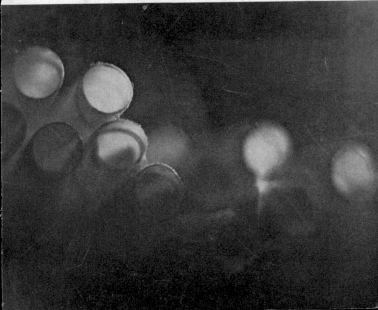

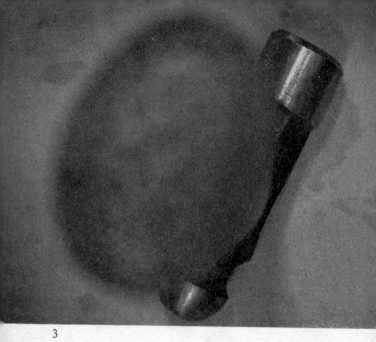

3

4

5

6

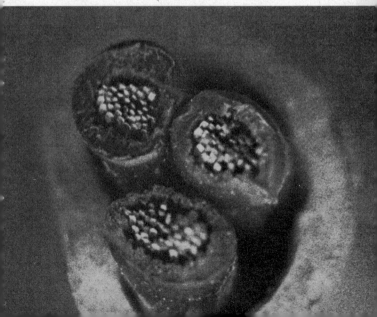

7

8

23 Chemistry

1 Thinking in terms of chemical elements, can you find the hidden ship in the expression: A – n ?

2 What do you get by fusing together sand, lime and soda?

3 What words do the chemical symbols for the following make: (a) carbon – oxygen – neon; (b) calcium – nitrogen; (c) hydrogen – aluminium – fluorine?

4 What is associated with these acids: (a) Formic acid, (b) Malic acid, (c) Citric acid, (d) Acetic acid?

5 Using chemical symbols for the elements, what is the word 'coins' composed of?

6 Which is the odd one out?
H_2SO_4 NaOH
HC1 HNO_3

7 Using chemical symbols for the elements, what would 'soap' be made of?

8 Two colourless solutions are mixed and as a result the mixture is densely clouded white. Which of the following would the solutions have been: (a) Copper sulphate and sodium carbonate, (b) Sodium carbonate and calcium nitrate, (c) Potassium chloride and calcium nitrate?

9 If the letters in the word 'fish' stand for the chemical elements, what is it made of?

10 What is the name given to the property of liquids that corresponds to friction in solids?

11 What is referred to in the following apothecary's recipe: Best ground Brazil wood 4 ounces; diluted with acetic acid, one pint: Alum, half an ounce. Boil the ingredients in an enamel vessel for one hour. Strain and add an ounce of gum and it is ready for use.

24 Poetry Quiz

1 In which play does this couplet begin the last speech:
  If we shadows have offended,
  Think but this, and all is mended?

2 What was the cargo of the 'quinquireme of Nineveh' in Masefield's poem?

3 To whom did the poet Lovelace address his verses on going to the war?

4 Of which poems are these the last lines: (a) *They also serve who only stand and wait,* (b) *If winter comes, can spring be far behind,* (c) *And gathering swallows twitter in the skies,* (d) *To strive, to seek, to find, and not to yield,* (e) *Far brighter than this gaudy melon flower?*

5 *Poor Johnny Brown*
  Is dead and gone
  We'll never see him no more
  For what he thought was H_2O . . . .
  Can you complete this rhyme?

6 Where does the following line occur: *But I kissed her little sister?*

7 What are the two preceding and the two succeeding lines of the following quotation:
  To sleep: perchance to dream: ay,
  *   there's the rub?*

8 In Milton's *Comus*, who sat under the 'glassy, cool, translucent wave'?

9 Alfred Lord Tennyson wrote about the Charge of the Light Brigade. He also wrote about the same campaign:
  But they rode like Victors and Lords
  Thro' the forest of lances and swords
  In the heart of the Russian hordes, . . .
  What was he describing?

10 *Have owre, have owre to Aberdour,*
  It's fifty fadom deip,
  And thair lies . . .
  Who?

11 What is the first line of this quotation:
  'Tis mightiest in the mightiest; it becomes
  The throned monarch better than his crown?

12 In the following quotations, what are the preceding lines:
(a) *We have no time to stand and stare,* (b) *Nor any drop to drink,* (c) *Walks the night in her silver shoon,* (d) *And day's at the morn?*

13 In Herrick's *Cherry Ripe*, whose lips are likened to the cherry?

14 *This be the verse you grave for me:*
   'Here he lies where he longed to be,
   Home is the sailor, home from the sea,
   What is the next line?

15 What are the preceding two lines and the following two lines of this quotation:
   The evil that men do lives after them,
   The good is oft interred with their bones?

16 What is the time in the following quotations: (a) *Cobbler, cobbler, mend my shoe, Get it done by . . .,* (b) *Past . . . on a cold frosty morning,* (c) *Stands the Church clock at . . . And is there honey still for tea?*

17 In what poem do the lines of the first verse end thus:
   day
   lea
   way
   me?

25 Places Near at Hand

1 Which four English counties start with D?

2 What is the missing town in the following sequence: Burslem, Hanley, Stoke and Tunstall?

3 The following locations in the British Isles are all in counties beginning with 'C': (a) Mount Snowdon, (b) Tintagel Castle, (c) John o'Groats, (d) Calder Hall Atomic Power Station, (e) Jodrell Bank. What are the counties?

4 In which city will you find: Petergate, Fishergate, Bootham Bar, Piccadilly and Whip-ma-wop-ma-gate?

5 How many geographical counties are there in: (a) England, (b) Scotland, (c) Wales, (d) Northern Ireland?

6 Apart from being English towns or cities, what have Bristol, Bath, Stratford and Salisbury in common?

7 The following towns are each in counties beginning with 'S': (a) Bridgnorth, (b) Woking, (c) Crewkerne, (d) Lichfield, (e) Bury St Edmunds. What are the counties?

8 Excluding London, in which city will you find the Royal Exchange, the Stock Exchange, Smithfield Market, Victoria Station and Piccadilly?

9 What have these names in common: Bailey, Plymouth, Thames, Fisher?

10 Travelling in a straight line from Derby to Peterborough, how many counties would you visit?

11 What are the English counties from Dover to Land's End?

12 Fourteen counties in Scotland have a county town or capital of the same name. Can you name six of them?

26 Musical Interlude

1 Tchaikovsky, Saint-Saëns and Sibelius each composed a piece of music about a bird. What was the bird and what were the pieces?

2 Who composed *Peter Grimes*?

3 Which composers had these Christian names: (a) Peter Ilyich, (b) Wolfgang Amadeus, (c) Christoph Willibald, (d) Georg Friedrich?

4 If there are eight notes in an octave and you play a two-octave scale up and down, how many notes do you play?

5 The Gilbert and Sullivan operas all have alternative and lesser known titles. What are the following better known as: (a) *The Slave of Duty*, (b) *Bunthorne's Bride*, (c) *Castle Adamant*, (d) *The King of Barataria*, (e) *The Witch's Curse*, (f) *The Merryman and his Maid*, (g) *The Peer and the Peri*, (h) *The Lass that Loved a Sailor*, (i) *The Town of Titipu*?

6 What is the opposite of *pizzicato*?

7 What piece of music is about a girl with enamel eyes?

8 Who wrote the Jupiter Symphony?

9 With which instruments do you associate: (a) Vladimir Ashkenazy, (b) Jacqueline du Pre, (c) Ravi Shankar?

10 Who composed the Brandenburg Concertos?

11 Which folk singer and guitarist was born in Minnesota on 24 May 1941 and has changed his name from Zimmerman?

12 Which composer is associated with fireworks and water?

13 Who wrote the symphony called 'The Planets'?

14 If grandfather is a bassoon, what is grandson?

15 Who wrote the Eroica Symphony?

27 General Knowledge 5

1 Which world-famous building carries the inscription over a tomb, 'Si monumentum requiris, circumspice', meaning 'If you seek his monument, look around', and to whom does the inscription refer?

2 Which day is associated with Odin's wife?

3 Where will you find the hammer, the anvil and the stirrup in one place?

4 If you ordered *Zuppa Inglese* (English soup) in an Italian restaurant, what would you get?

5 What does Britannia hold in her left hand on the 50p piece?

6 What gender do the following nouns take when translated into French: (a) Door, (b) Book, (c) Floor, (d) Ceiling?

7 What sort of information would you be looking for if you referred to: (a) Crockford, (b) Debrett, (c) Hansard, (d) Wisden?

8 What comes between the Scorpion and the Goat?

9 When would a ¾ Less Tyree follow Mark Twain?

10 If a Roman child prayed to Artemis and Ares, which names would he use?

11 Where would one find stocks, flettons and Staffordshire blues?

12 When Scotland was known as Caledonia, what was Ireland called?

13 Which British ship made its maiden voyage on 6 February 1886 and its last voyage in 1970?

14 A little Eskimo and a big Eskimo are walking in the snow. The little Eskimo is the big Eskimo's son. The big Eskimo is not the little Eskimo's father. How was this?

15 What are these and what does the crown denote?

28 Further Word Puzzles

1 SOHSATRRICKH.
Can you take away a fish and leave a bird?

2 BNRML.
Can you supply the vowels to make this a word?

3 Can you fill in the gaps by analogy?

LEFT	RIGHT	WRONG
EASY	?	SOFT
DARK	?	HEAVY

4 What do the abbreviations E.V.A. and A.L.S.E.P. stand for?

5 In this collection of 'cars', what 'car': (a) Wears a red hat, (b) Is red, and may be either valuable or painful, (c) Is a flower, (d) Is a merry occasion, (e) Is a spice from the East Indies, (f) Is a garment, (g) Is a mobile home?

6 Which word fits the space?

LOSE	(TILE)	PINT
IDES	(----)	BARD

7 What is unusual about this:
A MAN A PLAN A CANAL PANAMA?

8 Certain English words have the same spelling and pronunciation but different meanings. What are the words referred to in the following definitions: (a) A sword and a mark of ownership, (b) A handcart and a burial place, (c) A weapon and a dress accessory, (d) A doorkeeper and an alcoholic drink, (e) A scheme and a specified piece of land, (f) Two of a kind and a support?

9 What is the missing letter?
| A | D | H | M | ? |

10 What is significant about these words: 'innoculate', 'embarass', 'supercede', 'dessicate', 'rarify'?

11 Can you render intelligible this riddle found on a grave in Wales?
PRSVR Y PRFCT
    MN
VR KP THS PRCPTS
    TN

12 What is the significance of these letters:
    QWERTYUIOP
    ASDFGHJKL?

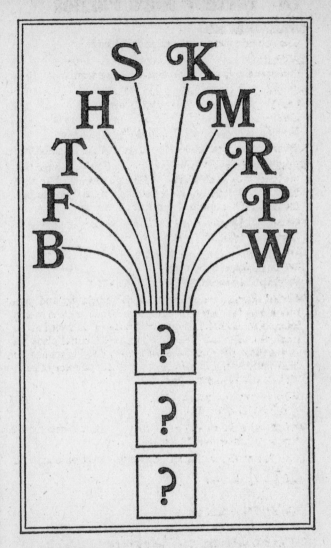

13 Which three letters fill the blanks to make a word from each initial consonant?

29 Nature Quiz

1 Which animal has extra long eyelashes, can close its nostrils and can drink as much as 25 gallons of water?

2 Which bird has a body which looks like a stork; eggs which look like those of a heron; and makes a noise in flight like a duck?

3 Can you complete the following to form the names of birds: (a) O - -, (b) - RE -, (c) - AR -, (d) - A - A -, (e) - O - C - N?

4 What swarm of insects is described as follows:
In May is worth a load of hay.
In June is worth a silver spoon.
In July is not worth a fly?

5 Which of these four fish is most likely to be found trapped in an iceberg: skate, perch, herring or halibut?

6 What is the fundamental difference between an ape and a monkey?

7 Which flower can be found in varieties of wild, China, cabbage, damask and moss?

8 What is a camelopard?

9 What are the three stages in a bee's life before it becomes fully fledged?

10 What sort of track would a bisulcate animal leave?

11 If you were told that there was a corniculate capriform quadruped in the garden, what would you expect to find?

12 Which of these creatures is a member of the order called
Orthoptera?

30 Number Quiz 5

1 A plant grows so that every morning the number of leaves doubles and every Wednesday and Thursday evening a quarter of the leaves are destroyed by frost. If there is one leaf on Sunday evening, how many will there will be the next Friday evening?

2 June's age last year was one year more than Julie's age this year. The sum of their ages is 14. How old are they?

3 Divide Ali Baba's thieves by the number of inches in a hand; multiply the result by the number of lines in a sonnet and divide it by the number of hills in Rome. What word describes the answer?

4 I have some marbles in each pocket. If I take two from my right pocket and put them in my left, I have equal amounts in each pocket. If I take two from my left and put them in my right I have five times as many in my right pocket as in my left. How many have I in each pocket?

5 If two numbers total 108 and one is three times the other, what are the numbers?

6 A party starts at 9 o'clock. Between 9 and 10 o'clock 30 people arrive. After 10, newcomers arrive at the rate of 25 an hour, while earlier comers leave at the rate of 15 an hour. How many people are at the party at midnight?

7 In three years a boy will be three times as old as he was three years ago. How old is he now?

8 What is the second letter after the midway letter between N and T?

9 'My husband's age,' remarked a lady, 'is represented by the figure of my own age reversed. He is my senior, and the difference between our ages is one eleventh of the sum of our ages.' How old is he?

10 When a barrel is half full of water, 12 gallons are poured into it making it two-thirds full. What is the barrel's capacity?

11 If NUMBER = 436721, what is $B + U \times R - N$?

12 What is the next number in the series?

13 Four actors have played the part of Tarzan in films over a period of years. The first appeared in two films and then each succeeding actor played the part twice as often as his predecessor. How many Tarzan films have been made?

14 How many 9-in.-square tiles are needed to cover a floor 7½ ft long by 6 ft wide?

15 A: *Twice as many eggs I'll eat as you*
    If you will give me two.
  B: *An equal number we shall get.*
    If I receive two from you.

    Twas thus two hungry men conversed
    How many eggs had each at first?

16 What are the missing numbers?
$$? \times 8 + 1 = 9$$
$$? \times 8 + 2 = 98$$
$$? \times 8 + 3 = 987$$
$$? \times 8 + 4 = 9876$$
$$? \times 8 + 5 = 98765$$

31 More People in Fact and Fiction

1 Where would you find the carpenter, the joiner, the weaver, the bellows mender, the tinker and the tailor, and what were their names?

2 Where were the homes of: (a) Dolly Daydream, (b) Polly Perkins, (c) Molly Malone?

3 What have these men in common: Charles Hamilton; Frank Richards; and Martin Clifford?

4 Who was the ferryman of the Styx and what was the name of his dog?

5 For what is Alexander Fleming famous?

6 To whom does the following information apply: he had four sisters and three brothers; one of his sisters was called Joan, and one of his brothers was called Gilbert; his elder child was called Susannah and his younger daughter Judith; he had a wife called Ann and a son called Hamnet?

7 W. S. Gilbert and A. S. Sullivan were associated in the production of comic operas. What names respectively does the initial 'S' stand for?

8 Under what other names are the following men known: (a) Mohammed Ali, (b) Samuel Clemens, (c) Edson Arantes do Nascimento?

9 Who followed little white stones and so reached their home?

10 Who went for a picnic and took: 'Cold tongue, cold ham, cold beef, pickled gherkins, salad, French rolls, cress sandwiches, potted meat, gingerbeer, lemonade, soda-water.'?

11 What was the relationship of Philip Pirrip to Joe Gargery?

12 What are the surnames in the following famous families: (a) Charlotte, Branwell, Anne, (b) Dingle, Michael, Hugh, (c) Thomas, Julian, Aldous, (d) John, Charles, Samuel, (e) John, Robert, Edward, (f) Leon, Eugene, Sidonie?

13 Who was known in India as 'Great Soul'?

32 All About Trees

1 Which tree wastes and dies?

2 Which tree is associated with cricket?

3 Which tree is neat and tidy?

4 Which tree is associated with a Canadian syrup?

5 Which tree keeps you warm?

6 Which tree is associated with ships?

7 Which tree can sweep?

8 Which tree is associated with a smithy?

9 Which tree is a residue?

10 Which tree is associated with archery?

11 Which tree occupies a governing position in a church?

Can you identify the following?   9

                                                   10

11

12

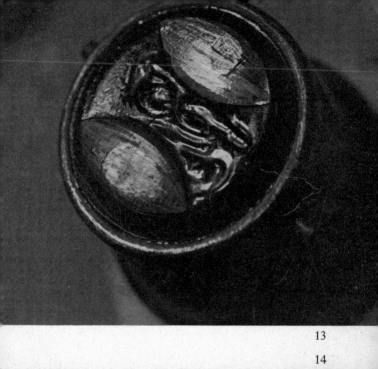

13

14

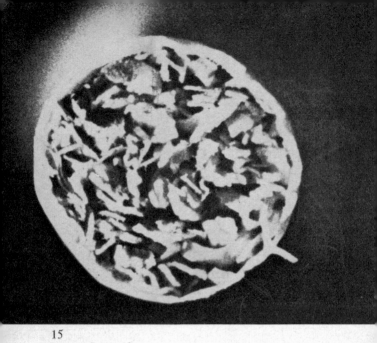

15

16

33 Literature 2

1 In what book are the principal characters Napoleon, Snowball and Boxer?

2 Can you complete the following titles of works by W. Somerset Maugham: (a) *The Fall of . . .*, (b) *The Vessel . . .*, (c) *The Hairless . . .*, (d) *The Three . . .*, (e) *Gigolo . . .*?

3 What are the following subtitles better known as: (a) *A Romance of Exmoor*, (b) *The Skeleton in the Cupboard*, (c) *The Weaver of Raveloe*, (d) *The Modern Prometheus*?

4 Of which famous novel is this the opening line: 'It is a truth universally acknowledged that a single man in possession of a good fortune must be in want of a wife . . .'?

5 In which of Shakespeare's plays do the following characters appear: (a) Valentine and Proteus, (b) Antonio, Bassanio and Lorenzo, (c) Perdita and Autolycus, (d) Reynaldo and Fortinbras?

6 Can you complete the following titles: (a) *The Last of Mrs . . .*, (b) *The Last of the . . .*, (c) *The Last Chronicle of . . .*?

7 Eric Blair was born in Bengal in 1903, brought to England at an early age and educated at Eton. What was his pen-name?

8 For what names do the initials of these famous writers stand: (a) H. G. Wells, (b) G. K. Chesterton, (c) P. G. Wodehouse, (d) Jerome K. Jerome, (e) J. B. Priestley?

9 What are the titles of the original plays from which these musical shows have been written: (a) *The Chocolate Soldier*, (b) *Man of La Mancha*, (c) *Catch my Soul*, (d) *Robert and Elizabeth*, (e) *Kiss Me Kate*, (f) *My Fair Lady*?

10 What story and its sequel has as its main characters the above animals?

1 What is the next name in this series: David, Fitzgerald, Baines?

2 Why is the name of the town Glenelg in Invernesshire unusual?

3 What lies on the seabed and trembles?

4 Who were Graceless, Pointless, Feckless and Aimless?

5 What is next in this series: Mercury, Venus, Earth, Mars, Jupiter?

6 Which famous Spanish painter is now living in France?

7 What is the connection between tumblers, pouters, runts and dragoons?

8 Where would you have found a couple of dozen of the species *Turdus merula* in strange culinary circumstances?

9 In my house I have a colour TV set and a black and white set. I use two transistor radios and one mains set. I also keep five dogs, all fully grown, and own a revolver. How many licences do I need?

10 If you have one match and you want to light a cigarette and the gas, which do you light first?

11 Which paw does the lion on the reverse side of the 10p piece have raised?

12 What is the link connecting these surnames: Allen, Castle, Kelly and Murray?

13 What is pinchbeck?

14 When translated into French, are the following words masculine or feminine: (a) 'Programme', (b) 'Profession', (c) 'Quality', (d) 'Restaurant', (e) 'Packet', (f) 'Paper'?

15 Can you name the last six Chancellors of the Exchequer?

16 What was cut short by the arrival of 'A person on business from Porlock'?

35 More Unlikely Connections

1 Which fastening can jump?

2 What do the following people have in common: The Duke of York; Dame Sybil Thorndike; Dame Peggy Ashcroft; Adeline Genée; Yvonne Arnaud; and Jeannetta Cochrane?

3 What is the connection between the City of Bath, the Lord Protector and Lionel Bart?

4 What is the connection between pop groups and: (a) A proverb, (b) Christmas decorations, (c) Expensive ladies' coats?

5 What insect is a game?

6 How are the names of the towns Wellington, Halifax, Stirling and Lancaster associated with World War II?

7 What have the following in common: Borodin's opera *Prince Igor*, Schubert's Eighth Symphony, and Dickens's *Edwin Drood*?

8 What have the following words in common: 'pie', 'new', 'row' and 'delta'?

9 What is the connection between a fruit and an appointment?

10 What sound do a stick, a garden and a group of people have in common?

11 What is the connection between Brown Turkey, White Marseilles, Black Ischia and Smyrna?

12 What have these in common?

36   Geographical Quiz 2

1 John is flying to Honolulu, Robert is flying to Tokyo. If they both start from London, who has the longer trip?

2 If from London Airport you travelled due east for 500 miles and from there 500 miles due south, which country would you be in?

3 What country is bordered by Peru, Brazil, Paraguay, Argentina and Chile?

4 If a man sailed due south from Land's End, where would he land?

5 What district of London is the capital of a Canadian province?

6 Where would you find these three mountain ranges: Macdonnell, Flinders and Great Dividing?

7 Where are: (a) The Golden Horn, (b) Cape Horn, (c) Little Big Horn?

8 The boundary between Canada and the United States runs through four of the five Great Lakes but the fifth is entirely in the United States. Which is it?

9 What six countries border France?

10 In which city could you go to Charing Cross, Hyde Park, Paddington and King's Cross via Double Bay?

11 Can you identify the following European countries from the approximate statistics of their area and population: (a) 30,000 square miles and 5 million people, (b) 50,000 square miles and 46 million people, (c) 116,000 square miles and 54 million people, (d) 174,000 square miles and 8 million people, (e) 213,000 square miles and 51 million people, (f) 195,000 square miles and 32 million people?

12 Which four American states are prefaced by the word 'new'?

37   Number Quiz 6

1 A man painting the walls and ceiling of a church suffers from a back ailment so that for every square yard he paints on the ceiling he has to paint one on the walls. If the four walls are 100 ft long and 20 ft high, which does he finish first?

2 A boy adds 130 to a certain number instead of subtracting it and his answer is 310. What should it have been?

3 The number 26 is made up of four whole numbers. If the highest number is twice the lowest and the other two are equal, what are they?

4 If you add the number of wheels on a gig to the number of wheels on a velocipede and subtract the wheels of a hansom cab, what answer to you get?

5 How many 'I's occur on a clock face with Roman numerals?

6 If you begin with the number of steps in Buchan's novel, divide by the number of men in a boat (J. K. Jerome), add the number of Pillars of Wisdom (T. E. Lawrence) and divide by the number of years before the mast (Richard Dana), what number is left?

7 If your stapler will staple ten cards together, how many will be needed to staple fifty together?

8 A man sold his car and gave half the money to his wife. He gave one-fifth to his eldest son, one-sixth to his second son, one-tenth to his daughter and the rest to his mother. If his mother received £40, how much was the car worth?

9 A Roman soldier was born in 80 BC. On his 25th birthday he fought in his first battle. Three years later he was promoted and sent north; two years after that he was again promoted and sent south. He returned to Rome eight years after his first battle. What year was that?

10 Can you fill in the arithmetical signs in the following:

$$9 \quad 7 \quad 4 = 4$$
$$9 \quad 7 \quad 4 = 67$$
$$9 \quad 7 \quad 4 = 6$$
$$9 \quad 7 \quad 4 = 8$$

11 Which is larger in terms of pears, an apple or a banana?

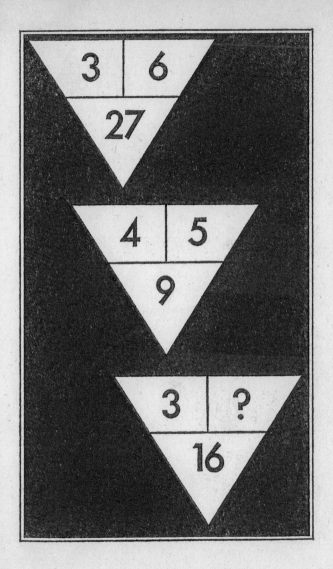

12 What is the missing number?

13 Three numbers total 70. If one number is half of one of the other numbers and twice as much as the other number, what is its value?

14 The average weight of three men A, B, and C, is 12½ stone. If A weighs 11 st. 6 lb., and B weighs 12st. 4 lb., what is C's weight?

15 Can you share £2.25 among A, B and C, giving B 25p less than A and C twice as much as B?

38 Questions of Colour

1 If red becomes brown, and black becomes blue, what does green become?

2 What colours are usually associated with Maria and Peter?

3 If you live at 1600 Pennsylvania Avenue, what is the colour of your house?

4 What comes between green and indigo?

5 If red goes east to west and black goes north to south, where does the yellow go?

6 Who went to sea 'in a beautiful pea-green boat'?

7 If you mix the colour in the name of the group who sing *Melting Pot* to the colour of the river that Christie sings about, you will get the first word, also a colour, of a song sung by Tom Jones. What is it?

8 What colours are: (a) The friendly cow, (b) My hen who lays eggs for gentlemen, (c) The Jumblies' hands?

9 What bird is pied, grey and blue-headed?

10 What colours are: (a) Maeterlinck's Bird, (b) Scott's Gauntlett, (c) Dumas's Tulip.

39 Yet More Word Puzzles

1 FABRICATION.
This word contains within itself, and with the letters in the right order, a word with the same meaning. What is it?

2 The words 'pots' and 'pans' have a similar meaning. Which single letter can be inserted into each word to give two other words with similar meanings?

3 GRREADEGBRNAEVRE.
Can you take away a tennis player and leave an actor?

4 What word means biscuits to the British; royalty to the French; and whisky to the Americans?

5 Which of the following words is mis-spelt: 'archiepiscopate', 'ecclesiasticism', 'sacerdotal', 'patriarcal'?

6 RDUETVLOANND.
Can you take away one English county and leave another?

7 Can you distinguish between 'antimony' and 'antinomy'?

8 What name is applicable to the following: (a) A domestic rodent, (b) A clergyman doing temporary duty, (c) A human being used as a subject for laboratory experiments?

9 If 7326154 equals TRAINED, what does 76232 equal?

10 In this collection of 'pets', which 'pet': (a) Is an article of clothing, (b) Is a rascally lawyer, (c) Is the study of rocks, (d) Is a sea-bird, (e) Is a supplication, (f) Is a flower?

11 Can you complete as a sentence:
                    A REST
                    UR?

12 What word represents: 'a surgical instrument', 'a magazine' and 'a style of window in architecture'?

                    XD   BL
                    ZH   ??
13 What comes next in this sequence?

7	T
26	A
18	I
15	L
12	O
9	R

14 What is this word?

40 General Knowledge 7

1 Taking 'John and Yoko' as an example, who is associated with: (a) Ringo, (b) George, (c) Paul, (d) Lulu?

2 Lepidodendron, sigillaria and calamites are found in coal seams. What are they?

3 Wire nails are measured in inches for their length and gauge for their thickness. Which would be the heavier of these two nails made from the same material: a nail 1½ in. long and gauge 8, or a nail 1½ in. long and gauge 14?

4 If $\frac{6}{8}$ gives you 2, and $\frac{3}{4}$ gives you 3, what does C give you?

5 If you were given 'Gammer Gurton's Needle', what would you do with it?

6 What would you take for catching gwyniad-vendace or powan?

7 Who in mythology was the first woman on earth shaped according to Zeus so that her charm and beauty should bring misery to mankind?

8 What is the next word in the following sequence: Andrew, Benjamin, Charlie, David, –?

9 What is the significance of the word 'salt' in the expression 'to be worth one's salt'?

10 If a man finds it difficult to walk, which of these bones would he have broken: (a) Ulna, (b) Tibia, (c) Scapula, (d) Humerus?

11 Which island would you be on if the main department stores included Macy's, Gimbels, Saks and Bloomingdales?

12 Who is missing from this list: *Les Parapluies*, *Guernica*, *Sunflowers*, Renoir, Van Gogh?

13 Can you complete this quotation from Lord Acton: 'Power tends to corrupt . . .'

14 Who founded the Oxford College, Christ Church?

15 What organisation was founded by the Swiss banker, Henri Dunant?

16 Which Italian painter is famous for his royal portraits?

17 Where would you find the words: 'Pity Me', 'Bothwell', 'Idle' and 'Ugley'?

Answers

1 General Knowledge 1

1 Derbyshire. The Duke of Norfolk's seat is Arundel Castle, Sussex, and the Duke of Devonshire's is Chatsworth House, Derbyshire.

2 Philadelphia, founded by William Penn as a Quaker Colony.

3 A Hi-Fi speaker. 'Wow' is distortion in reproduced sound; 'flutter' is higher pitched distortion. 'Tweeter' is a small loudspeaker reproducing sounds of high pitch and 'woofer' is a loudspeaker reproducing sounds of low pitch.

4 By visiting *H.M.S. Belfast*, in the Pool of London. She is the largest cruiser ever built for the Royal Navy and the last remaining big gun ship.

5 In a collection of ferns. *Davallia canariensis* is Hare's Foot fern, and *Platycerium* is Stag's Head fern.

6 Wildfell Hall. (*The Tenant of Wildfell Hall* by Anne Brontë, published under the pseudonuim of Acton Bell.)

7 (a) and (b) Salisbury Cathedral, 8,760 and 365 respectively. When the cathedral was built there were also doors for every month of the year.

8 Acton. (John Emerich Edward Dalberg Acton, first Baron Acton, 1834-1902, was an English historian and brilliant scholar. He was Professor of Modern History at Cambridge from 1895-1902.)

9 The Republic of San Marino in Italy.

10 Nelson. His statue is 17 ft 4 in. and the column is 184 ft 10 in.

11 Ramsey. They were Archbishops of Canterbury. (Randall Thomas Davidson was Archbishop from 1903-28; Cosmo Gordon Lang 1928-42; William Temple 1942-44; Geoffrey Francis Fisher 1945-61; Arthur Michael Ramsey 1961 –.)

12 The Battle of Waterloo on 18 June 1815. Copenhagen was the name of Wellington's horse; Marengo was Napoleon's horse.

13 They are forms of the pansy (the common name of viola), a word derived from the French *pensée*, a thought.

14 Wandsworth Bridge, which is between Battersea and Putney Bridges.

2 Number Quiz 1

1 1, 2, 3.

2 Small.

3 (c). $\left(\dfrac{1,764}{14} = 126.\right)$

4 70 yards. $(4 \times 12' \ 6'' = 50'$
$\quad\quad\quad\quad\quad\ \ 6 \times 14' \ 4'' = 86'$
$\quad\quad\quad\quad\quad\ \ 8 \times \ \ 9' \ 3'' = 74'$

$\quad\quad\quad\quad\quad\quad\quad\ \ 210' = 70 \text{ yards.})$

5 H (not counting Q itself).

6 $8\frac{8}{9}$. (1 mile $= \frac{8}{5}$ kilometres; 1 gallon $= 4.5$ litres.)

7 29. $(15-13) \times 11 + 7 = 29$. (Rugby Union has 15 players a side; Rugby League has 13; Association Football has 11, and the ages of man are 7 in Jacques' speech in *As You Like It* – *His acts being seven ages*.)

8 Twice. (July and August; December and January.)

9 Two o'clock.

10 12 ft. (21 rungs make 20 spaces. 20×6 in. $= 10$ ft $+2$ ft $= 12$ ft.)

11 £57.

12 3.

13 Three years.

14 49. Take away one figure from the other in the bottom circles and square the answer.

15 550 2-ft-square turfs.

3 Some Word Games

1 Vienna – Austria.

2 Chesterfield. (a) The Fourth Earl of Chesterfield, who wrote *Letters to his Son*, published in 1774.

3 'Rain', 'reign' and 'rein'.

4 (a) 'Bathos'. (b) 'Batting', (c) 'Batter', (d) 'Batman'.

5 'Peer' and 'pier'.

6 'Skillfull' should be 'skilful'.

7 U– 'ewe', 'you' and 'yew'.

8 UNP. (ABD = 'bad', 'dab'. DNO = 'nod', 'don'. SWA = 'was', 'saw'. IPN = 'pin', 'nip'. UNP = 'pun'.)

9 Ashen.

10 Take away Picasso and leave Matisse.

11 A cardinal.

12 Kowloon (Hong Kong), and monsoon.

13 Q. There are always three letters between them horizontally or vertically.

14 'Untied'.

15 (a) 'Catamaran'. (b) 'Catapult'. (c) 'Catastrophe'.

16 They retain the old English 'en' in the plural.

4   People in Fact and Fiction

1 (a) Darling. *Peter Pan* by J. M. Barrie. (b) Sawyer. *Tom Sawyer* by Mark Twain. (c) Robinson. *The Swiss Family Robinson* by Johann Rudolph Wyss.

2 Meg, Jo, Beth and Amy March, the four sisters in *Little Women* by Louisa M. Alcott.

3 Paris, a young nobleman in *Romeo and Juliet* and a son of Priam in *Troilus and Cressida*.

4 Neil Armstrong on 20 July 1969, when he stepped on to the moon.

5 (a) Bysshe (English poet). (b) Simpson (American general, later 18th President of the USA). (c) Tecumseh (American general).

6 In Trafalgar Square, London. Nelson was made Duke of Brontë in 1799. Sir Edwin Henry Landseer (1802-73), animal painter, modelled the lions for the Nelson monument.

7 Zebedee. (Zebedee Tring in *The Archers*.)

8 Robert Frost (1874-1963) and C. P. Snow (born in 1905).

9 Anne, Queen of Louis XIII, gave them to Buckingham in *The Three Musketeers* by Alexandre Dumas.

10 (a) A companion of Robin Hood. (b) A Justice of the Peace in Shakespeare's *The Merry Wives of Windsor*, and *Henry IV, Parts i and ii*. (c) A beetle, one of Rabbit's friends-and-relations from *The House at Pooh Corner* by A. A. Milne.

11 (a) William Ewart Gladstone, (b) Samuel Langhorne Clemens (Mark Twain), (c) Charles Lutwidge Dodgson (Lewis Carroll), (d) Oscar Fingall O'Flahertie Wills Wilde.

12 Little Jack Horner – 'What a good boy am I!'

13 (a) Collins (astronauts). (b) Japhet (sons of Noah). (c) Mary (a group of folk singers). (d) Nod (characters in a nursery poem by Eugene Field).

14 He pioneered the use of antiseptics in surgery.

15 (a) El Cid. (b) Beauclerc or Scholar. (c) Marshal Tito. (d) Joseph Stalin.

16 A golden pear, in the nursery rhyme *I had a little nut tree*.

17 Three (or four if Baby Bear was female).

18 The Unknown Warrior. His tomb is in Westminster Abbey.

5 Geographical Quiz

1 Northern Ireland (Fermanagh, Antrim, Tyrone, London-derry, Armagh, Down).

2 New York.

3 Newfoundland, Canada.

4 (c).

5 Gitchee Gumee. The quotation is from Longfellow's *Hiawatha*.

6 The Cape of Good Hope.

7 Antarctica.

8 Yugoslavia.

9 Ontario, Canada.

10 Antarctica.

11 Amsterdam. Dublin is 279 miles, Amsterdam 231 miles.

12 Jamaica.

13 The Netherlands.

14 Nairobi – 4,331 miles. (Bermuda is 3,430 miles and Toronto 3,547 miles.)

6 General Knowledge 2

1 Eat them. They are all varieties of plum.

2 The standard gauge on British Railways. George Stevenson built his first rail to 4 ft. 8½ ins.

3 Michelangelo.

4 (a) A coloured neckscarf, as worn by Jim Belcher, the prize-fighter (1781-1811). (b) A short over-jacket designed by the third Earl Spencer, worn at the end of the 18th century. The name also refers to a close-fitting bodice worn by women in the early 19th century. (c) A soft felt hat with indented crown, named after the heroine of *Trilby* by George du Maurier.

5 (a) Rowing takes 1,140 calories; running 975, and bicycling 660.

6 They are varieties of gooseberry.

7 The Three Fates of Greek mythology.

8 (a) The Allied landings in North Africa in 1943. (b) The German plan for the invasion of Britain in 1940. (c) The Allied landings in June 1944 in Normandy. (d) The construction of prefabricated ports to follow the D-Day landings.

9 Groups of stars.

10 1 March – St David's Day. The other dates are St Patrick's Day; St George's Day and St Andrew's Day, the patron saints of Ireland, England and Scotland respectively.

11 (a) Hot Chocolate, (b) Middle of the Road, (c) Marmalade.

12 Mandarin Chinese.

13 The two countries had different calendars. England used the Julian calendar and Spain the Gregorian calendar.

14 An apple.

15 It depends on which way you are going.

16 Clifton Suspension Bridge, Clifton, Bristol.

7 Anagrams

1 Somerset (W. Somerset Maugham).

2 Testimonial.

3 Punishment.

4 Centenarian.

5 Madrigals. ('Melodious birds sing madrigals' from *The Passionate Shepherd to his Love* by Christopher Marlowe.)

6 Schoolmaster.

7 Penitentiary.

8 A shoplifter.

9 Vegetarianism.

10 Houses of Parliament.

11 George Best.

12 Parishioners.

13 Mathematics.

14 Oudenarde. (Battle won by Marlborough against the French on 11 July 1708.)

8 Number Quiz 2

1 33 (12+3+4+3+2+9). The 12 Apostles in the New Testament; *The Three Musketeers* by Alexandre Dumas; *Four Just Men* by Edgar Wallace, the Three Stooges, a film comedy trio; the two lily white boys in *Green Grow the Rushes O*, and the nine ladies dancing in *The Twelve Days of Christmas*.

2 Four.

3 126. (21 on each, therefore 21 × 6 = 126).

4 A twelfth.

5 60. (11 + 13 + 17 + 19 = 60).

6 15 and 45.

7 3600 square yards. If one side is 180 yards less than 4 sides, 3 sides must equal 180 yards. One side must therefore be 60 yards long. 60 × 60 = 3600.

8 Two minutes. They all flash together every 24 seconds.

9 $\frac{5}{8}$.

10 4 (1942).

11 Twelve old pence equals five new pence.

12 Due west.　D　A
　　　　　　 C　B

13　1　　　2
　　3　　　4
　　6　　　5
　　8　　　7
　　—　　　—
　　18　　 18

14 Pineapple = 10p; banana = 20p, and pear = 30p.

15 16. The numbers add up to 10, 20, 30 and 40.

16 Thursday. St George's day is 23 April.

17 36 seconds. 176 = 1/10 mile, and 1/10 mile at 10 mph takes 1/1000 hour = 36 seconds.

9　Odd Man Out

1 (d). Lloyd George is a type of raspberry; the others are apples.

2 Ruby. It is an inorganic gem whilst all the others are organic gems.

3 Sweden. It is the only flag which does not consist of three plainly coloured horizontal stripes.

4 Hezekiah is not a book of the Bible, but the others are.

5 Etna because it is the only volcano of the four mountains.

6 Faeroes because they belong to Denmark, not Britain.

7 The dahlia, because it grows from a tuberous root not a bulb. (Also, the tulip, hyacinth and daffodil normally bloom in the spring months, and the dahlia in summer and autumn.)

10 More Word Games

1 'See' and 'sea'.

2 A bathysphere is let down on a cable from the side of a ship, and can be controlled only by its parent cable, but a bathyscaphe is capable of diving and rising under its own power and can move horizontally. They are both submersible vessels for deep-sea observation.

3 (a) Defence of the Realm Act. (b) Entertainments National Service Association. (c) Navy, Army and Air Force Institutes. (d) Officer Cadet Training Unit. (e) Pipe line under the ocean. (f) Radio detection and ranging.

4 'Rite', 'write' and 'right'.

5 Teams.

6 'Atlas'.

7 They all contain 'pter'. (A 'pterodactyl' is a prehistoric winged reptile.)

8 Kyoto and Tokyo.

9 Ample.

10 'Meet', 'meat', and 'mete'.

11 (a) Hoity toity (an exclamation of contempt at unduly assuming behaviour), (b) Hokey pokey (cheating), (or Wakey wakey!), (c) Hoi polloi (the rabble).

12 'Fast', 'easy', 'mass', 'last', 'ease', 'vase', 'wasp', 'base', 'case', 'lass', 'mast', 'cast', 'past', etc.

13 (a) *Id est* – that is. (b) *Exempli gratia* – by way of example. (c) *Videlicet* – namely, that is. (d) *Quod vide* – which see.

14 (a) 'Collaborate'. (b) 'Collateral'. (c) 'Collusion'.

15 'Bark' and 'barque'.

16 Ramadan and Matapan. Ramadan is the ninth month of the Mohammedan year and is observed as a 30 days' fast during daylight. Matapan was a battle between the British and Italian fleets off Cape Matapan in Greece in 1941.

11 Religious Quiz

1 Epiphany and Christmas.

2 Job and Lot.

3 The Archbishop of York who is known as *Ebor*, the Latin for York.

4 (b). St Paul's Epistle to Titus.

5 Samson. He slew his victims with the jawbone of an ass.

6 Arthur Michael Ramsey, Archbishop of Canterbury.

7 Deuteronomy.

8 Aaron.

9 John Wesley, in his *Journal* for 1739.

10 Malta – then known as Melita.

12 General Knowledge 3

1 C.H. (Confederation Helvetia). The Swiss use these initials to avoid confusion with Sweden, which uses S.

2 (a) Lord Avon, (b) Winston S. Churchill, (c) Harold Macmillan.

3 Vermicelli.

4 Father.

5 Varieties of strawberry.

6 It is the examination of coins (cupro-nickel, gold and silver) by a jury entirely independent of the Mint. It is a procedure in accordance with the Coinage Acts of 1870-1946 to ensure the proper weight and composition of the coins. The trial is annual and is held by the Goldsmiths' Company of the City of London. Pyx chest is where the coins are put before the trial.

7 (a) Mosaic. (b) Etching.

8 Willow pattern china ware, popular for almost two centuries in England. It was introduced by Thomas Turner at the Caughley pottery, Shropshire, between 1775-80.

9 Laurence Stephen Lowry, born in 1887, who painted the Lancashire industrial scene.

10 Brian, who saw the flash, was first. Charles, who saw the bullet strike the water, was second, whilst Andrew, who heard the report, was last.

11 Paul Gaugin (1848-1903).

12 They are fictional names, in 19th-century novels, for the real towns of Knutsford, Dorchester and Brussels. The novels are: *Cranford* by Mrs Gaskell, *The Mayor of Casterbridge* by Thomas Hardy and *Villette* by Charlotte Brontë.

13 Z.

14 They are all types of butterfly.

15 James Abbott McNeill Whistler (1834-1903).

16 They were all fighter aircraft built by Hawkers in World War II.

17 They are all names of Haydn symphonies. The Oxford Symphony is No. 92; the London No. 104; the Hen No. 83; the Clock No. 101 and the Miracle No. 102 (originally No. 96).

13 Literature

1 Mr and Mrs Snagsby, who are characters in *Bleak House* by Charles Dickens. The others are in *The Pickwick Papers*.

2 (a) Titania (*A Midsummer Night's Dream*). (b) Octavia (*Antony and Cleopatra*). (c) Calpurnia (*Julius Caesar*). (d) Desdemona (*Othello*). (e) Hermione (*The Winter's Tale*).

3 Baroness Orczy. She wrote *The Scarlet Pimpernel*, published in 1905, and its sequels.

4 Francis Durbridge (Paul Temple); Agatha Christie (Miss Marple and Hercule Poirot); Leslie Charteris (Simon Templar), and John Creasey (Gideon of the Yard and the Baron).

5 (a) Anne's pseudonym was Acton Bell. (b) Charlotte's was Currer Bell. (c) Emily's was Ellis Bell.

6 (a) Hugh Walpole, *Rogue Herries*, *Judith Paris* and *The Fortress*, (b) John Galsworthy, *The Forsyte Saga*. (c) Louisa M. Alcott, *Little Women*, *Good Wives*, *Jo's Boys* and *Little Men*. (d) Dornford Yates (the pseudonym of Cecil William Mercer).

7 (a) Max de Winter in *Rebecca* by Daphne du Maurier. (b) The Brontës. (c) Eliza Doolittle in *Pygmalion* by George Bernard Shaw.

8 W. Somerset Maugham.

9 (a) *Indefatigable* by C. S. Forester, one of the Hornblower series. (b) *Vanity Fair* by William Makepeace Thackeray. (c) *Treasure Island* by Robert Louis Stevenson.

10 Agatha Christie. *Passenger to Frankfurt* was published in 1971. (The number includes six books published under her pseudonym, Mary Westmaycott.)

11 (a) Bulwer Lytton, published in 1834. (b) Washington Irving (his pseudonym was Geoffrey Crayon), published in 1820. (c) Oliver Goldsmith, produced in 1773. (d) Richard Barham, published in 1840.

14 Kings and Queens

1 Charles II (1660-85). The Plague was in 1665 and the Fire in 1666.

2 Ten months, from January to October 1066.

3 Wat Tyler and Richard II, during the Peasants' Revolt.

4 (a) Henry II (1154-89) and Richard II (1377-99); (b) Henry VII (1485-1509) and Elizabeth I (1558-1603); (c) George I (1714-27) and Victoria (1837-1901).

5 (a) George V in 1893. (b) James II in 1673 (his second marriage). (c) Charles II in 1662. (d) Queen Anne in 1683.

6 (a) Grandfather and grandson. (b) Uncle and niece.

7 Queen Victoria (1837-1901). The American Civil War lasted from 12 April 1861 to 9 April 1865.

8 Mary, Queen of Scots.

9 Mary I, 1553-58; Elizabeth I, 1558-1603; Mary II, 1689-94; Anne, 1702-14; Victoria, 1837-1901. All were Queens Regnant.

10 Richard II (1377-99); Henry IV (1399-1413); Henry V (1413-22) and Henry VI (1422-61).

11 Katharine of Aragon, Anne Boleyn, Jane Seymour, Anne of Cleeves, Catherine Howard, Catherine Parr.

12 William I (The Conqueror) 1066-1087; William II (William Rufus) 1087-1100; Henry I 1100-1135; Stephen 1135-1154.

13 Harthacanute, 1040-42, and Edward the Confessor, 1042-66.

14 Both were proclaimed king but never crowned. Edward V was (reputedly) murdered in the Tower. Edward VIII was proclaimed king in 1936 and abdicated in 1936.

15   Number Quiz 3

1 7.

2 2,400 lbs.

3 None.

4 5 and 35.

5 Bill.

6 Sixty sweets can be divided equally among any number up to six.

7 One minute. The distance travelled is $770 \frac{1}{3} + 10 = 880$ yds. $= \frac{1}{2}$ mile. A train travelling at 30 mph takes one minute to travel half a mile.

8 None.

9 110.

10 288.

11 Never.
   Thirty days hath September,
   April!, June and November.

12 None. $4 \times 50 = 200 = 40\%$ of 500. Hence the total 40% are already in the four planes.

13 $4\frac{1}{2}$ laps. $30 \times 1\frac{1}{2} = 45$ minutes $= 4\frac{1}{2}$ laps.

14 24. Add the top two numbers and divide by 3.

15 5 – the root of the difference between the bottom two numbers.

16 8.

17 63. Nine apples per day, 63 per week.

16 History

1 Sir William Wallace, executed for treason.

2 Blenheim. The poem is *The Battle of Blenheim* by Robert Southey (1744-1843), the battle was fought in 1704.

3 The Great Fire of London of 1666.

4 Guinevere. They are pairs of English monarchs and their consorts: Victoria and Albert; Edward VII and Alexandra; Lionheart (Richard I) and Berengaria, and Arthur and Guinevere.

5 (b). Shakespeare died in 1616. The respective dates of the other events are 1215, 1815 and 1715.

6 Sir George Downing (1623-84), soldier and politician.

7 The Act forbidding the wearing of the kilt.

8 Raglan and cardigan. (A raglan was originally an overcoat with sleeves designed to go over the shoulder. The name now more generally describes this style of sleeve.)

9 They were unmarried.

10 (a) Henry IV (1403). (b) Henry VI (1431). (c) Richard II (1381).

11 York and Lancaster. The sequence should be Norman, Plantagenet, Lancaster, York, Tudor etc.

12 Catherine the Great of Russia (1729-96).

13 They were decisive battles in the English Civil War. Naseby was in 1645; Edge Hill in 1642 and Marston Moor in 1644.

14 (a) 1745. (b) 1415. (c) 1805. (d) 1651. (e) 1805.

15 Six: Winston S. Churchill, Anthony Eden, Harold Macmillan, Alec Douglas-Home, Harold Wilson and Edward Heath.

16 1900.

17 Sporting Interlude

1 Baseball. ('Bean ball' is when the ball is thrown at a player's head by mistake. 'Charley Horse' means a player's expression after pulling a muscle. The term applies in other sports too. 'Foot in the bucket' means not standing properly to receive the ball.)

2 The Scottish Second Division has 19 teams.

3 27 points. (Brown 4+green 3+yellow 2+blue 5+pink 6+black 7=27).

4 Queen's Park Rangers (Queen's Park and Rangers).

5 All were captains of their own teams.

6 (a) Rugby. (b) Boxing. (c) Horse Trials. (d) Tennis. (e) Baseball.

7 A black belt (Judo).

8 Rowing; swimming (backstroke) and tug-of-war.

9 (a) Yachting. (b) Tennis. (c) Rugby. (d) Racing.

10 (a) Cockfighting. (b) Mexico.

11 (a) The Wallabies. (b) The All Blacks. (c) The Lions.

12 (a) Nine. (b) Twelve (ten in the U.S.A. and Canada). (c) Seven.

13 (a) Archery. (b) Baseball. (c) Hockey. (d) Rugby football. (e) All-in wrestling.

14 Hockey.

15 Sheffield Wednesday would be playing Newcastle United at the home of Leeds United, Elland Road, Leeds. (The Owls are Sheffield Wednesday; the Magpies are Newcastle United and the Peacocks are Leeds United.)

16 They are all 'saints'. The Southampton team is called 'The Saints'; Perth 'St Johnstone'; Paisley 'St Mirren' and Simon Templar is the Saint in the Leslie Charteris detective stories.

18 More Anagrams

1 Bonfire Night.

2 Shadow Cabinet.

3 Makepeace (William Makepeace Thackeray).

4 Mediterranean.

5 Mount Everest.

6 Hire purchase.

7 Advertisement.

8 Marriage.

9 Christening.

10 Dyspepsia.

11 Parsimonious.

12 St Pancras Station.

13 The solar system.

19   River Quiz

1 Alph in *Kubla Khan* by Samuel Taylor Coleridge.

2 The Wash.

3 The Thames, in *Prothalamion* by Edmund Spenser.

4 The Weser, which washes the walls of Hamelin in *The Pied Piper of Hamelin* by Robert Browning.

5 The Mississippi, in *Huckleberry Finn* by Mark Twain.

6 The Severn.

7 The Jordan, in the spiritual *One More River to Cross*.

8 The Dee. From the song *The Miller of Dee*.

9 The Don – *And Quiet Flows the Don* by M. Sholokhov.

10 The Limpopo in 'How the Elephant Got Its Trunk' from *The Just-so Stories* by Rudyard Kipling.

11 (a) Switzerland. (b) Germany. (c) Turkey. (d) Peru.

20   General Knowledge 4

1 Winston S. Churchill.

2 (a) Madrid. (b) Amsterdam. (c) Florence. (d) New York.

3 (a) White poppies. (b) Cinchona bark. (c) Coca leaves.

4 Proxima Centauri, 4.28 light-years away.

5 Hilaire Germain Edgard Degas (1834-1917).

6 (a) Belgium. (b) Australia. (c) The Netherlands. (d) Scandinavia. (e) Israel. (f) USSR.

7 The 13 stripes on the US flag represent the 13 original states which defeated George III in the War of American Independence in 1777.

8 When a pianist plays Chopin's 'Minute Waltz'.

9 A jury.

10 The procedure by which a debate in the House of Commons can be cut short despite the wish of the minority to continue it.

11 Seaweed.

12 The ship's name.

13 These were the names given to two Russian dogs sent into orbit.

14 Château d'If. The list is of famous prisons and prisoners. Oscar Wilde – Reading Gaol; Rudolf Hess – Spandau; Lt Col. Dreyfus – Devil's Island; Edmund Dantés – Château d'If.

21 Unlikely Connections

1 Jersey and Bikini. (Bikini Atoll is one of the Marshall Islands in the South Pacific.)

2 Hispaniola, which comprises Haiti and the Dominican Republic, in the Greater Antilles. It is also the name of the schooner in *Treasure Island.*

3 (a) They both wrote diaries. (b) They were both destroyed on their maiden voyage. (c) They were both blind. (Pew was the blind buccaneer in R. L. Stevenson's *Treasure Island.*)

4 They were all types of Victorian chairs.

5 Milton Keynes, the new city to be built in Buckinghamshire. (John Milton, 1608-74 and John Maynard Keynes, 1883-1946.)

6 Perch (measure of $5\frac{1}{2}$ yards, and freshwater fish).

7 Herringbone. (Architecture – zigzag pattern of stones or tiles in masonry. Carpentry – herringbone bridging. Cloth – cross-stitch in tweed.)

8 Bismarck.

9 Squash (game and soft drink).

10 They are all types of bread loaves.

11 Beech.

12 Bunyan. (John Bunyan 1628-1688.)

13 The shoes are plimsolls, and the Plimsoll line was adopted in 1876 as the safety mark for the loading of ships.

22 Number Quiz 4

1 20 minutes.

2 (a) 32 (3+3+24+1+1). (b) 78 (12+12+48+2+4).

3 They both take the same time – 50 seconds.

4 36. (V + VI + VII + VIII + X = 36.)

5 $2\frac{1}{2}$.

6 $\frac{3}{4}$ inch. $(10 \times \frac{1}{4}'') - (7 \times \frac{1}{4}'') = \frac{3}{4}$ inch.

7 192 (256 − 64).

8 Thursday.

9 45.

10 33 ft. 30 mph represents a distance of 44 ft per second.

11 The old second. There are only 86,400 of these to the day compared with 100,000 new ones.

12 $2\frac{1}{2}$p.

13 20 minutes.

14 Top = 128 (multiply the numbers across).
Bottom = 24 (add the numbers across).

15 3.

23 Chemistry

1 *Argo*. (A = argon (an inert gas), therefore A − n = Argo.)

2 Window glass.

3 (a) 'Cone' – C, O, Ne. (b) 'Can' – Ca, N. (c) 'Half' – H, Al, F.

4 (a) Ants (contained in a fluid emitted by them). (b) Apples and other fruits. (c) Oranges, lemons, grapefruit, limes, etc. (d) Vinegar.

5 Carbon (C), oxygen (O), iodine (I), nitrogen (N), and sulphur (S).

6 NaOH (caustic soda). It is an alkali and the others are acids. H_2SO_4 is sulphuric acid; HC1 is hydrochloric acid and HNO_3 is nitric acid.

7 Sulphur (S), oxygen (O), argon (A) and phosphorous (P).

8 (b). (a) is blue and (c) would still be colourless, unless a very strong mixture.

9 Fluorine (F), iodine (I), sulphur (S) and hydrogen (H).

10 Viscosity.

11 Red writing ink.

24 Poetry Quiz

1 *A Midsummer Night's Dream* by William Shakespeare. The speech is spoken by Puck.

2 Ivory, apes, peacocks, sandalwood, cedarwood and sweet white wine, in *Cargoes* by John Masefield.

3 Lucasta, in *To Lucasta, going to the wars* by Richard Lovelace (1618-58).

4 (a) *On His Blindness* by John Milton. (b) *Ode to the West Wind* by Percy Bysshe Shelley. (c) *Ode to Autumn* by John Keats. (d) *Ulysses* by Alfred Lord Tennyson. (e) *Home Thoughts from Abroad* by Robert Browning.

5 *Was really* H_2SO_4. (H_2O = hydroxide = water; H_2SO_4 = sulphuric acid.)

6 In the song *Clementine* by Percy Montrose. The next line is: *And forgot my Clementine.*

7 The preceding lines are:
That flesh is heir to, 'tis a consummation
Devoutly to be wish'd. To die, to sleep;
The succeeding lines are:
For in that sleep of death what dreams may come
When we have shuffled off this mortal coil.
The quotation is from *Hamlet* by William Shakespeare.

8 Sabrina.

9 *The Charge of the Heavy Brigade at Balaclava.*

10 . . . *guid Sir Patrick Spens*
Wi' the Scots lords at his feit.
(The eighteenth-century Scots ballad *Sir Patrick Spens*.)

11 *The quality of mercy is not strain'd*, Portia's speech in *The Merchant of Venice* by William Shakespeare.

12 (a) *What is this life if, full of care,* (from *Leisure* by W. H. Davies). (b) *Water, water everywhere* (from *The Rime of the Ancient Mariner* by S. T. Coleridge). (c) *Slowly, silently, now the moon* (from *Silver* by Walter de la Mare). (d) *The year's at the spring* (from *Pippa Passes* by Robert Browning).

13 Julia – *Where my Julia's lips doe smile.*

14 *And the hunter home from the hill.* This is from *Requiem* by Robert Louis Stevenson.

15 The preceding two lines are:
Friends, Romans, countrymen, lend me your ears;
I come to bury Caesar, not to praise him.
The following two lines are:
So let it be with Caesar. The noble Brutus
Hath told you Caesar was ambitious;
The quotation is from *Julius Caesar* by William Shakespeare.

16 (a) Half-past two. (Nursery rhyme.) (b) Three o'clock. (Christmas Carol.) (c) Ten to three. (*The Old Vicarage, Grantchester* by Rupert Brooke.)

17 *Elegy Written in a Country Churchyard* by Thomas Gray.
The curfew tolls the knell of parting day,
The lowing herd wind slowly o'er the lea,
The plowman homeward plods his weary way,
And leaves the world to darkness and to me.

25 Places Near at Hand

1 Durham, Dorset, Derbyshire and Devon.

2 Longton. The Five Towns of the Potteries, in Staffordshire, of which Arnold Bennett wrote.

3 (a) Caernarvon. (b) Cornwall. (c) Caithness. (d) Cumberland. (e) Cheshire.

4 York.

5 (a) 40. (b) 33. (c) 12. (d) 6.

6 A River Avon.

7 (a) Shropshire. (b) Surrey. (c) Somerset. (d) Staffordshire. (e) Suffolk.

8 Manchester.

9 They are the names of areas around the British Isles used in shipping forecasts.

10 Five. (Derbyshire, Nottinghamshire, Leicestershire, Rutland and Northamptonshire.)

11 Kent, Sussex, Hampshire, Dorset, Devon and Cornwall.

12 Aberdeen, Ayr, Banff, Dunbarton, Dumfries, Inverness, Kinross, Kirkudbright, Nairn, Peebles, Perth, Selkirk, Stirling, and Wigtown.

26 Musical Interlude

1 The swan. *Swan Lake* by Tchaikovsky; *The Swans* by Saint-Saëns; and *The Swan of Tuonela* by Sibelius.

2 Benjamin Britten.

3 (a) Tchaikovsky. (b) Mozart. (c) Gluck. (d) Handel.

4 29.

5 (a) *The Pirates of Penzance.* (b) *Patience.* (c) *Princess Ida.* (d) *The Gondoliers.* (e) *Ruddigore.* (f) *The Yeomen of the Guard.* (g) *Iolanthe.* (h) *H.M.S. Pinafore.* (i) *The Mikado.*

6 *Arco.*

7 The ballet *Coppélia* by Delibes.

8 Wolfgang Amadeus Mozart.

9 (a) Pianoforte. (b) Cello. (c) Sitar.

10 Johann Sebastian Bach.

11 Bob Dylan, who changed his name in honour of the Welsh poet Dylan Thomas.

12 Georg Friedrich Handel, who composed *Water Music* and *Music for the Royal Fireworks*.

13 Gustav Holst.

14 A string quartet, which represents Peter in Prokofiev's *Peter and the Wolf*.

15 Ludwig van Beethoven.

27 General Knowledge 5

1 St Paul's Cathedral, London. The inscription refers to the architect, Sir Christopher Wren.

2 Friday. It was called after Friga or Frea, wife of Odin, the chief deity of Norse mythology.

3 In the human ear. They are the three small bones between the eardrum and the organ of hearing.

4 Trifle.

5 An olive branch.

6 (a) Feminine – *la porte*. (b) Masculine – *le livre*. (c) Masculine – *le plancher*. (d) Masculine – *le plafond*.

7 (a) Clergy list. (b) The Peerage. (c) Parliamentary debates. (d) Cricket.

8 The Archer. They are signs of the zodiac. The Scorpion is Scorpio, the Archer is Sagittarius and the Goat is Capricorn.

9 On a Mississippi River Boat. They are calls of depth: Mark Twain equals 12 ft, ¾ Less Tyree equals 16½ ft.

10 Diana and Mars. Diana was the huntress and goddess of chastity and the moon. Mars was the god of war.

11 In a building. They are all types of brick.

12 Hibernia.

13 *S.S. Great Britain*, which returned to Britain on 23 June 1970.

14 She was his mother.

15 They are London silver hallmarks. The crowned leopard's head denotes silver made before 1829 and the uncrowned head silver made after this.

28 Further Word Puzzles

1 Shark – Ostrich.

2 Abnormal.

3 Hard – Light.

4 Extra Vehicular Activity and Apollo Lunar Surface Experiment Package.

5 (a) 'Cardinal'. (b) 'Carbuncle'. (c) 'Carnation'. (d) 'Carnival'. (e) 'Cardamon'. (f) 'Cardigan'. (g) 'Caravan'.

6 Dais.

7 It is a palindrome.

8 (a) Brand. (b) Barrow. (c) Bow. (d) Porter. (e) Plot. (f) Brace.

9 S. There are 2, 3, 4 and 5 letters respectively between those in the figure.

10 They all have one spelling mistake except 'dessicate' which has two. (Spellings should be 'inoculate', 'embarrass', 'supersede', 'desiccate' and 'rarefy'.)

11 Add E.   Persevere ye perfect men
            Ever keep these precepts ten. (It applies to the Ten Commandments.)

12 They are the second and third rows on a typewriter keyboard.

13 *ill* or *ail*.

29 Nature Quiz

1 The camel.

2 The flamingo.

3 (a) Owl. (b) Wren. (c) Lark. (d) Macaw. (e) Toucan.

4 A swarm of bees. An anonymous rhyme found in *The Oxford Dictionary of Quotations*.

5 Perch. Icebergs are fresh-water and the other three are salt-water fish.

6 Apes have no tails. Gorillas, chimpanzees, orangoutangs, and gibbons are apes.

7 The rose.

8 A giraffe. (It is also a constellation situated between Ursa Major and Cassiopeia.)

9 Egg, larva and pupa.

10 The mark of a cloven hoof.

11 A goat with horns.

12 The cockroach.

30 Number Quiz 5

1 18.

2 June is 8 and Julie is 6.

3 Score = 20. (40 thieves, 4 inches, 14 lines and 7 hills.)

4 I have eight in my right pocket and four in my left.

5 81 and 27.

6 50. (30+2(25-15).)

7 Six.

8 S. (Q is the midway letter, therefore S is the second letter.)

9 54.

10 72 gallons. ($\frac{2}{3}-\frac{1}{2}=\frac{1}{6}$=12 gallons. 6×12=72.)

11 7+3×1−4=6.

12 125. They are the cubes of 1, 2, 3, 4 and 5 respectively.

13 30. (2+4+8+16=30.)

14 80.

15 14 and 10.

16     $1 \times 8 + 1 = 9$
    $12 \times 8 + 2 = 98$
    $123 \times 8 + 3 = 987$
    $1234 \times 8 + 4 = 9876$
    $12345 \times 8 + 5 = 98765.$

31   More People in Fact and Fiction

1 They are the Players in *A Midsummer Night's Dream*. Their names are: Peter Quince (carpenter), Snug (joiner), Bottom (weaver), Flute (bellows mender), Tom Snout (tinker) and Robin Starveling (tailor).

2 (a) Idaho. (b) Paddington Green. (c) Dublin. (They are all in folk-songs.)

3 They are all the same person. Charles Hamilton wrote his stories for boys (Billy Bunter series) in the *Magnet* under the pen-name of Martin Clifford and in the *Gem* under the pen-name of Frank Richards.

4 Charon was the ferryman and Cerberus his dog. In Greek mythology the River Styx was in Hades and the shades of the departed were ferried over it.

5 The discovery of penicillin in 1928.

6 William Shakespeare.

7 Schwenk and Seymour.

8 (a) Cassius Clay (world heavyweight boxing champion).
(b) Mark Twain (American author). (c) Pele (Brazilian footballer).

9 Hansel and Gretel.

10 Mole and Ratty in *The Wind in the Willows* by Kenneth Grahame, published in 1908.

11 Brother-in-law. Joe married Pip's sister in *Great Expectations* by Charles Dickens.

12 (a) Brontë. (b) Foot. (c) Huxley. (d) Wesley. (e) Kennedy. (f) Goossens.

13 'Mahatma' Gandhi, 1869-1948. ('Mahatma' means Great Soul.)

32 All About Trees

1 The pine.

2 The willow, from which bats are made.

3 The spruce.

4 The maple.

5 The fir.

6 The oak.

7 Broom.

8 The chestnut.

9 The ash.

10 The yew.

11 The elder.

33 Literature 2

1 *Animal Farm* by George Orwell, published in 1945. Napoleon represents Stalin; Snowball represents Trotsky, and Boxer represents the strength, simplicity and good nature of the common man.

2 (a) . . . *Edward Barnard.* (b) . . . *of Wrath.* (c) . . . *Mexican.*
(d) . . . *Fat Women of Antibes.*
(e) . . . *and Gigolette.*

3 (a) *Lorna Doone* by R. D. Blackmore. (b) *Cakes and Ale* by W. Somerset Maugham. (c) *Silas Marner* by George Eliot. (d) *Frankenstein* by Mary Shelley.

4 *Pride and Prejudice* by Jane Austen.

5 (a) *The Two Gentlemen of Verona.* (b) *The Merchant of Venice.* (c) *The Winter's Tale.* (d) *Hamlet, Prince of Denmark.*

6 (a) . . . *Cheyney* by Frederick Lonsdale. (b) . . . *Mohicans* by Fenimore Cooper. (c) . . . *Barset* by Anthony Trollope.

7 George Orwell (1903-50).

8 (a) Herbert George. (b) Gilbert Keith. (c) Pelham Grenville. (d) Klapka. (e) John Boynton.

9 (a) *Arms and the Man* by George Bernard Shaw. (b) *Don Quixote* by Cervantes. (c) *Othello* by William Shakespeare. (d) *The Barretts of Wimpole Street* by Rudolph Besier. (e) *The Taming of the Shrew* by William Shakespeare. (f) *Pygmalion* by George Bernard Shaw.

10 *Winnie the Pooh* by A. A. Milne, published in 1926, and *The House at Pooh Corner* published in 1928.

34 General Knowledge 6

1 Milhaus. They are the middle names of the last four American Presidents: Dwight David Eisenhower; John Fitzgerald Kennedy; Lyndon Baines Johnson and Richard Milhaus Nixon.

2 It is a palindrome. (There are also two rivers and a town of the same name in Australia.)

3 A nervous wreck.

4 The cows in *Cold Comfort Farm* by Stella Gibbons published in 1932.

5 Saturn. They are all planets going outwards from the sun.

6 Pablo Picasso, born in 1881.

7 They are all breeds of pigeons.

8 Four and twenty blackbirds baked in a pie.

9 Seven. One for the colour TV covers the other TV, five for the dogs and one firearms licence. Radios no longer require a licence.

10 The match.

11 The right front paw.

12 Barbara.

13 A gold-like alloy of copper and zinc used in cheap jewellery.

14 (a) Masculine: *le programme*. (b) Feminine: *la profession*.
(c) Feminine: *la qualité*. (d) Masculine: *le restaurant*.
(e) Masculine: *le paquet*. (f) Masculine: *le papier*.

15 Anthony Barber, Iain MacLeod, Roy Jenkins, James Callaghan, Reginald Maudling and Selwyn Lloyd.

16 The poem *Kubla Khan*, a fragment by Samuel Taylor Coleridge, published in 1816.

35 More Unlikely Connections

1 Frog (a military coat fastening of spindle-shaped button and loop and an amphibious animal).

2 They all have theatres named after them. (The Duke of York's Theatre is in London; the Thorndike Theatre in Leatherhead; the Ashcroft Theatre in Croydon; the Adeline Genée Theatre in East Grinstead; the Arnaud Theatre in Guildford and the Cochrane Theatre in London.)

3 Oliver. Bath olivers (biscuits which originated in Bath), Oliver Cromwell, and the musical *Oliver* by Lionel Bart from Dickens' *Oliver Twist*.

4 (a) The Rolling Stones ('A rolling stone gathers no moss').
(b) The Hollies. (c) The Blue Mink.

5 Cricket (insect and game).

6 They were all the names of bombers.

7 They were all unfinished by their original authors.

8 They have the same sounds as four Greek letters.

9 Date.

10 Q – 'cue', 'Kew' and 'queue'.

11 They are all types of fig.

12 Each is the largest species of its class: the elephant is the largest land mammal; the albatross is the largest sea bird; the whale is the largest sea mammal and the ostrich is the largest land bird.

36 Geographical Quiz 2

1 Robert. Honolulu is 8,418 miles from London by air and Tokyo is 8,995 miles.

2 Italy, between Bologna and Florence. Germany would be 500 miles east of London Airport.

3 Bolivia.

4 Spain.

5 Edmonton, the provincial capital of Alberta, and a residential suburb of North London.

6 Australia. Macdonnell Range is in the Northern Territory; the Flinders Range is in South Australia and the Great Dividing Range runs north to south from Queensland to Victoria.

7 (a) Istanbul. It is a peninsula on the Bosporus forming the harbour of Istanbul. (b) Chile – the southernmost point of South America. (c) USA. It is a river which rises in Wyoming and flows to Montana.

8 Lake Michigan.

9 Belgium, Luxemburg, Switzerland, Germany, Spain and Italy.

10 Sydney, Australia. (Double Bay is a suburb of Sydney; Charing Cross is an intersection; Hyde Park is a park; Paddington and King's Cross are suburbs of Sydney.)

11 (a) Scotland. (b) England. (c) Italy. (d) Sweden. (e) France. (f) Spain.

12 New Mexico, New Hampshire, New Jersey, New York.

37 Number Quiz 6

1 The walls. (Area of ceiling = $100' \times 100' = 10,000$ sq. ft. Area of walls = $4 \times 100' \times 20' = 8,000$ sq. ft.)

2 50.

3 8, 7, 7, 4.

4 Two. All three vehicles have two wheels.

5 Usually 17 (I, II, III, IV, VI, VII, VIII, IX, XI, XII), but sometimes 20 when 4 is IIII.

6 10. (39÷3+7÷2). *The Thirty-nine Steps* by John Buchan;
Three Men in a Boat by Jerome K. Jerome; *Seven Pillars of
Wisdom* by T. E. Lawrence and *Two Years Before the Mast*
by Richard Dana.

7 Six.

8 £1,200.　　　600 to wife
　　　　　　　240 to eldest son
　　　　　　　200 to second son
　　　　　　　120 to daughter
　　　　　　　　40 to mother
　　　　　　　 ─────
　　　　　　　1,200

9 47 BC. (80−25=55−8=47.)

10 9+7÷4= 4
　　9×7+4=67
　　9−7+4= 6
　　9−7×4= 8

11 An apple. (1 apple=2 pears, 1 banana=1 pear).

12 5. Square the top numbers and subtract one from the other.

13 20. (20+10+40=70.)

14 13 st. 11 lb.

15 A gets 75p. B gets 50p. and C gets 100p.

38　Questions of Colour

1 Green and yellow stripes. They are the new colours of
insulation on electric plugs. (Brown=live, blue=neutral,
green and yellow=earth.)

2 Black and blue. Black Maria, the prison van; and Blue
Peter, the flag flown when a ship is about to sail.

3 White. This is the address of 'The White House', the
official residence of the President of the USA.

4 Blue – in the colours of the spectrum.

5 Round in a circle (London Transport map). Red refers to
the Central Line, black to the Northern Line and yellow to
the Circle Line.

6 The Owl and the Pussycat (Edward Lear).

7 Green. (Blue Mink, *Yellow River* and *The Green, Green Grass of Home*.)

8 (a) Red and white (from *A Child's Garden of Verses* by R. L. Stevenson). (b) black (*Hicketty, picketty my black hen* —traditional nursery rhyme). (c) blue (from *The Jumblies* by Edward Lear).

9 The wagtail.

10 (a) Blue, (b) red, (c) black.

39 Yet More Word Puzzles

1 'Fiction'.

2 L – 'plots' and 'plans'.

3 Clark GRAEBNER and Michael REDGRAVE.

4 'Bourbon'. (Bourbon biscuits were first made in 1910 in London. The Bourbons were a branch of the French royal family. To Americans Bourbon is rye whisky.)

5 'Patriarcal' should be 'patriarchal'.

6 Rutland – Devon.

7 'Antimony' is a metallic element. 'Antinomy' is a contradiction in a law.

8 'Guinea pig'.

9 Tiara.

10 (a) 'Petticoat'. (b) 'Pettifogger'. (c) 'Petrology'. (d) 'Petrel'. (e) 'Petition'. (f) 'Petunia'.

11 You are under arrest.

12 'Lancet'.

13 DP. The first is the next letter but one, and the second has three letters intervening.

14 Tailor.

1 (a) Maureen (Starr). (b) Patti (Harrison). (c) Linda (McCartney). (d) Maurice (Gibb).

2 Plant fossils.

3 The first nail. The higher the gauge, the thinner the nail.

4 4. $\frac{6}{8}$ gives 2 beats in a bar; $\frac{3}{4}$ gives 3, while C is written for common time – 4 beats in a bar.

5 Read or act it. It is the second English verse comedy, published in 1575.

6 Fishing tackle.

7 Pandora.

8 Edward. This is the phonetic alphabet.

9 In Roman times salt was very precious and soldiers were given an allowance to buy salt. This was called *salarium* (salt-money) and from it comes our word 'salary'.

10 (b) – the shinbone. (Ulna is the forearm, scapula the shoulder blade and humerus the upper arm.)

11 Manhattan, New York.

12 Picasso. They are pairs of paintings and painters: Renoir painted *Les Parapluies*, Van Gogh, *Sunflowers* and Picasso, *Guernica*.

13 . . . and absolute power corrupts absolutely.

14 Cardinal Wolsey.

15 The Red Cross, in 1863.

16 Pietro Annigoni, born in 1910.

17 On a map. They are all place names. Pity Me is in Durham, Bothwell is in Lanarkshire, Idle in Yorkshire, and Ugley in Essex.

Answers to Photo Quiz

(*between pages* 48-49)

1 Deck-chair.

2 Drinking straws.

3 Hammer – looking down as it is raised.

4 Spout of watering can.

5 Pepper corns.

6 End of three-core wire flex.

7 Packet of frankfurter sausages.

8 Pile of fifty-penny pieces.

9 Rose thorn.

10 Phillips' screw-heads.

11 Tea bag.

12 Battery socket.

13 End of light bulb.

14 Pack of cards.

15 End of cigarette.

16 Pine cones.

Two other popular quiz books based on BBC programmes.

Quiz Ball

Since 1966 when BBC TV's first **Quiz Ball** programme was shown, the majority of Britain's top soccer players have had the opportunity of showing their skill off the field by answering sporting and general knowledge questions. The book contains hundreds of questions (and answers) arranged so that Quiz Ball can be played at home.   30p

Brain of Britain

For over twenty years a general knowledge quiz written and devised by John P. Wynn has been a regular feature on British and overseas radio programmes.

This book, with over eight hundred questions (and their answers) arranged in subject quizzes, reflects the tremendous diversity of the programme. It will provide hours of enjoyment for quiz enthusiasts and for the young and not-so-young who want to improve their general knowledge.   35p